7 Secrets of Highly Effective Social Impact Communicators

How to Grow Your Influence to Solve Society's Most Pressing Challenges

Nate Birt

Apress®

7 Secrets of Highly Effective Social Impact Communicators: How to Grow Your Influence to Solve Society's Most Pressing Challenges

Nate Birt
High Hill, MO, USA

ISBN-13 (pbk): 978-1-4842-9797-1 ISBN-13 (electronic): 978-1-4842-9798-8
https://doi.org/10.1007/978-1-4842-9798-8

Copyright © 2023 by Nate Birt

This work is subject to copyright. All rights are reserved by the Publisher, whether the whole or part of the material is concerned, specifically the rights of translation, reprinting, reuse of illustrations, recitation, broadcasting, reproduction on microfilms or in any other physical way, and transmission or information storage and retrieval, electronic adaptation, computer software, or by similar or dissimilar methodology now known or hereafter developed.

Trademarked names, logos, and images may appear in this book. Rather than use a trademark symbol with every occurrence of a trademarked name, logo, or image we use the names, logos, and images only in an editorial fashion and to the benefit of the trademark owner, with no intention of infringement of the trademark.

The use in this publication of trade names, trademarks, service marks, and similar terms, even if they are not identified as such, is not to be taken as an expression of opinion as to whether or not they are subject to proprietary rights.

While the advice and information in this book are believed to be true and accurate at the date of publication, neither the authors nor the editors nor the publisher can accept any legal responsibility for any errors or omissions that may be made. The publisher makes no warranty, express or implied, with respect to the material contained herein.

    Managing Director, Apress Media LLC: Welmoed Spahr
    Acquisitions Editor: Shivangi Ramachandran
    Development Editor: James Markham
    Coordinating Editor: Shaul Elson

Cover designed by eStudioCalamar

Distributed to the book trade worldwide by Apress Media, LLC, 1 New York Plaza, New York, NY 10004, U.S.A. Phone 1-800-SPRINGER, fax (201) 348-4505, e-mail orders-ny@springer-sbm.com, or visit www.springeronline.com. Apress Media, LLC is a California LLC and the sole member (owner) is Springer Science + Business Media Finance Inc (SSBM Finance Inc). SSBM Finance Inc is a **Delaware** corporation.

For information on translations, please e-mail booktranslations@springernature.com; for reprint, paperback, or audio rights, please e-mail bookpermissions@springernature.com.

Apress titles may be purchased in bulk for academic, corporate, or promotional use. eBook versions and licenses are also available for most titles. For more information, reference our Print and eBook Bulk Sales web page at http://www.apress.com/bulk-sales.

Any source code or other supplementary material referenced by the author in this book is available to readers on GitHub (https://github.com/Apress). For more detailed information, please visit https://www.apress.com/gp/services/source-code.

Paper in this product is recyclable

This book is dedicated to all my friends at Farm Journal. You took this suburban kid under your wing, put him in dirty boots, and turned him into a farm boy capable of doing hard work and helping others. Thank you.

Table of Contents

About the Author xiii

About the Technical Reviewer xv

Acknowledgments xvii

Introduction xix

Chapter 1: Secret #1: Highly effective social impact communicators ... care both about the words and the mission 1

Define the mission and why it matters to you 3

A word about technical skill 6

Harness the power of purpose 7

Curiosity drives you to keep discovering new facets of the mission 9

    Part 1: Commit nothing to memory save impressions and a handful of key insights 10

    Part 2: Do your homework about that social impact issue 11

    Part 3: Ask experts directly to fully understand the context 11

Know yourself best to be the best mission-bearer 14

Practical ways to put your social impact mission before the words you use 16

    1. Understand what's at stake 17

    2. Understand what's at risk 17

    3. Crave a brighter world with better opportunities 18

    4. Feel compelled to bring others alongside you 20

    5. Fuse communication and leadership together 21

TABLE OF CONTENTS

    6. Clarify your vision and talk about it 22

        The mission reminds you social impact is achievable 23

  Key Questions 24

Chapter 2: Secret #2: Highly effective social impact communicators ... are astute translators inside and outside of their organizations 25

Navigate friction with the future in mind 26

Get comfortable standing out as a translator 28

Why social impact communicators must learn to translate among parties—and how 30

    ... Understand and recognize the worldviews and unique sectoral cultures of different stakeholder types 31

    ... See both sides of an issue 33

    ... Explain a complex issue in ways many can understand 36

    ... Define your personal views on the social impact issues you help solve 38

    ... Build the most compelling case in partnership with others 40

    ... Stay humble and stay focused on the mission 41

    ... Mold exactly the right team for the work you're doing 43

    ... Achieve diverse social impact outcomes across different industries amid rapid change 45

    ... Find a home within your organization and among your peers at last 46

How translation has served my social impact journey so far 47

Key Questions 48

Chapter 3: Secret #3: Highly effective social impact communicators ... leverage the strength of personal and organizational values to tell compelling stories 49

The place where values come from is the workshop inside your head—and inside your organization 51

What power do values really have? 57

Define the solutions you offer as a social impact communicator 61
    Writing 61
    Editing 61
    Facilitating 62
    Leading 62
    Empowering 62
    Building 63

Want to be more effective? Pair the right value(s) to the right social impact solutions.. 63

Why you must keep adding values to your toolbox.. 67

But what if you encounter a situation where your values could be compromised? 68

Define your "actions accompanying values"—when X happens, I will do Y 70

What to do when values conflict: Understand, align as possible, and influence 72

Learn to discover others' values quickly—and work toward them together...... 73

Embrace a bigger worldview than you thought possible 74

Key Questions 75

Chapter 4: Secret #4: Highly effective social impact communicators ... embrace the renewable fuel of teamwork............77

Burnout is real in social impact communication, even though we're so focused on the mission we ignore it... 80

Strategies for strengthening your social impact team by reversing the status quo 82

    Status quo: Conduct meetings that crush the soul............................... 84
    Your choice: Conduct meetings that embolden and launch.................. 84
    Status quo: Cast a vision only you can see 85
    Your choice: Co-create your vision with your team 85
    Status quo: Set deadlines impossible from the word "go"..................... 85

TABLE OF CONTENTS

- Your choice: Set realistic and flexible deadlines 86
- Status quo: Treat people like commodities—all alike 86
- Your choice: Put people first, work together, and make something great 87
- Status quo: Celebrate statistics only, not accompanying success stories 87
- Your choice: Celebrate stories of impact underpinned by data 88
- How to foster a mindful and impactful team using the PURSUE framework 88

When the going gets tough, turn to daily micro habits to get unstuck and get going 93
- Micro Habit #1: Great teams embrace the work and one another, flaws and all 95
- Micro Habit #2: Great teams overpower the isolation and misunderstood nature of social impact work 96
- Micro Habit #3: Great teams know one another personally as well as professionally 98
- Micro Habit #4: Great teams draw energy from complementary capabilities 99
- Micro Habit #5: Great teams show gratitude before attitude—there's nothing to prove until you have something to prove 101
- Micro Habit #6: Great teams navigate complexity with calm, not chaos..... 102
- Micro Habit #7: Great teams seek cohesion rather than full clarity—people feel part of something great, even external partners 104
- Micro Habit #8: Great teams champion honesty, admit when things could be better, and work to make it so 105

Teamwork is only renewable to the extent you invest in it 107

Key Questions 108

Chapter 5: Secret #5: Highly effective social impact communicators ... reframe every setback as the crest of a hill 109

- New insights yield new direction—and the potential for disorienting doubt ... 111
- Crest-climbing insight No. 1: Hills provide unprecedented perspective 115

TABLE OF CONTENTS

Crest-climbing insight No. 2: Each hill must be tackled differently, though there are patterns 116

Crest-climbing insight No. 3: Once you've defined what's hard, you can determine what's possible 118

Crest-climbing insight No. 4: Your flawed fear needs a free ride home 120

Crest-climbing insight No. 5: You can't climb all the hills today 121

Great social impact communicators build a resilient mindset to keep going in the face of adversity 122

    Act with integrity 124

    Lead with humility 125

    Be scientific in your approach 125

    Stay skeptical 126

    Communicate with transparency and openness 127

After your hike past the crest, learn to navigate the cloud forest beyond 129

    <u>W</u>ait 130

    <u>A</u>nalyze 131

    <u>T</u>ake Gratitude 131

    <u>E</u>valuate Options 132

    <u>R</u>un Again 132

The watchout and the opportunity 133

Key Questions 134

Chapter 6: Secret #6: Highly effective social impact communicators … cede perfection to the messy reality of change-making 135

How messy looks for social impact communicators 137

Paint the vision, not Van Gogh 139

Why you should embrace satisfied persistence rather than perfection 141

    Stop trying to tie up all the loose ends 143

TABLE OF CONTENTS

    Move ahead instead of around in circles..144

    When the dust flies, remember it will settle...149

    Capture attention and direct focus rather than sowing chaos 152

    Turn panic into peaceful action 154

    Guard the silent moments 156

    Engage in regular conversation that sparks ideas and opportunities 159

Trade predictability for adaptability 161

Key Questions 162

Chapter 7: Secret #7: Highly effective social impact communicators ... build personal and professional legacies that outlive them and their careers..163

First principles of legacy building for social impact communicators 165

    Principle No. 1: Legacy is the ripple effect of our actions 166

    Principle No. 2: Legacy is shiftable, not set in stone 167

    Principle No. 3: Legacy exists beyond our lifetime....................................168

    Principle No. 4: Legacy can be a blessing or a byword 168

    Principle No. 5: Legacy persists in the background 169

How you can create a legacy that outlives you...170

    Legacy Builder 1: Give away your grace and mercy liberally 171

    Legacy Builder 2: Guard your time and share it so it aligns with your values and the mission..173

    Legacy Builder 3: Be honest with yourself and others about who you really are..174

    Legacy Builder 4: Focus on actions that hold true 500 years from now......175

    Legacy Builder 5: Seek forgiveness over apologies 177

    Legacy Builder 6: Be slow yet deliberate, not fast and reckless 178

    Legacy Builder 7: Bring trusted partners into your inner circle..................179

    Legacy Builder 8: Help others remember the promise of their own multigenerational dream 180

TABLE OF CONTENTS

Ask the experts: How can social impact communicators build personal and professional legacies that outlive them and their careers?........................ 181

Some final thoughts on legacy and the journey before you............................... 183

Key Questions 187

Chapter 8: Some helpful resources for social impact communicators..189

Recommended Reading 191

Index...193

About the Author

Nate Birt is a nationally published author, speaker, and founder of Silver Maple Strategies (www.SilverMapleStrategies.com), a social impact communication consulting company. He helps purpose-driven executives accelerate massive goals through content strategy, grant proposal development, and private coaching. Nate is a senior adviser to Trust In Food, the mission-driven division of Farm Journal focused on accelerating the adoption of climate-smart agriculture. He has helped organizations build and implement multimillion-dollar climate change programs across Fortune 500 companies, global nonprofits, and government agencies. Nate holds a master's in journalism from the University of Missouri. His writing has appeared in the *Detroit Free Press*, *Entrepreneur*, *Fast Company*, and *The Washington Post*. He and his wife, Julie, operate a small farm with their four children—Micah, Titus, Ezra, and Phoebe—outside of St. Louis.

About the Technical Reviewer

Over the course of a 25-year career spanning Fortune 500 companies, nonprofits, and foundations, **Amy Skoczlas Cole** has worked to reimagine the systems that deliver sustainable food, clean water, and low carbon energy to society. She serves as President of Trust In Food, Farm Journal's mission-driven division focused on accelerating the adoption of climate-smart agriculture. Previously, she has led groundbreaking social impact change efforts at eBay, American Public Media, and Pentair. She started her career at Conservation International, where she forged some of the earliest partnerships between environmentalists and the private sector.

Acknowledgments

I am so grateful to everyone who made this book for purpose-driven communicators possible. I'd first like to thank Shiva Ramachandran at Apress. She immediately expressed excitement about the topic, coached me at every stage of publication, and redoubled my belief in the power of books to clarify our thinking and transform our hearts for good. Likewise I am forever grateful to Shon Vareichung, who shepherded me and this volume—and kept me on deadline. I extend deepest thankfulness and friendship to this book's technical reviewer, Amy Skoczlas Cole, for her generous investment of time, compassion, and a critical eye toward the core themes, framing, and explanation of the concepts in this book. Without her contributions amid an extraordinarily full executive plate, this book would have fallen flat on the shelf—and I along with it. Sincere thanks to the experts who generously gave of their time and insights for the interviews found in the second half of this book: Martín Casanova, Max Gulde, Kent Harrison, and Deron Johnson. You are a credit to your profession and are leaving a powerful legacy any communicator would do well to follow. Last but not least, I am blessed beyond measure to count my wife, Julie, and my children—Micah, Titus, Ezra, and Phoebe—as my biggest champions, encouragers, and pop-up camper trekking companions. Thank you all for believing in me, even when I fail to believe in myself. I would thank our dogs, chickens, turkeys, and dairy cows, but there are too many of them to name. And anyway, they don't know how to read.

Introduction

What is (and isn't) social impact communication?

An awkward conversation during my daughter's ballet class led me to this project. It all began so innocently.

There I was, seated on a slick blue couch that, for its lack of a back, at least offered padding (thank heaven for small comforts). Another dad and I struck up a conversation.

"What do you do?" I asked.

He explained his work as an attorney who handled an array of cases including family law and criminal cases.

"What do you do?" he replied.

"I'm a social impact consultant," I replied.

He sat there for a split second. Dazed and confused.

"What does that mean?" he asked.

From here, I tap-danced (or perhaps pirouetted—this was, after all, a ballet class) my way down a rather slippery slope and into safely tangible territory. I talked about how my background is in food and agriculture. I spoke about environmental stewardship—helping farmers build soil health and water quality. I explained that my specialty happens to be communication strategy and content creation.

Then, I turned the conversation back to lawyers, a favorite and beloved profession from time immemorial.

You should not have to face a similar fate. The humiliation of confused stares. The genuinely interested yet befuddled family, friends, and neighbors who feel they'll never know what to do with what you do.

INTRODUCTION

The personal defeat of winnowing your social impact mastercraft to a job title: a writer, a strategist, and so on.

This book is about helping you get clear on what social impact communication is—and is not—so that you grow your impact, your influence, and make a multigenerational mark on the world.

You are helping to define a discipline from the ground up. And I am here to teach you what I have learned along the way about social impact communication. Let me explain how I am qualified to help you before you race to the nearest bookstore shelf and exchange this volume for the Brothers Grimm or the latest Nordic noir.

About me and my background as a social impact communicator

I am both a student and a practitioner of social impact communication. After graduating from the world's oldest journalism school at the University of Missouri, I embarked on a career in media. I ran the newsroom in the Missouri River community of Boonville and covered two St. Louis suburbs for what was then AOL's Patch.com brand.

I had fun, met interesting people, told compelling (and sometimes controversial) stories.

Then, I got burned out. I needed a change. Through a serendipitous LinkedIn search, my wife, Julie, discovered that a college friend worked at a prestigious business-to-business (B2B) company in the food and agriculture industry. I ended up spending the next decade in this extraordinary field—and learning many of the social impact communications lessons I'll share in this book.

In October 2022, I transitioned into my own full-time social impact communication consulting business, Silver Maple Strategies. I wanted to take more time for my family, as we homeschool our children on our small Missouri farm. And I wanted to reimagine how I could be a champion for the very social impact communication work I'd come to love.

INTRODUCTION

What social impact communication is and is not

My first order of business is to remind you, my fellow social impact communicator, that you matter. The work you are doing can be challenging. I am hopeful I can help make your day-to-day communication work a bit easier by providing a framework for what you do. It is both new and inclusive of many types of communication professionals while also encompassing the classical disciplines on which it draws so heavily—disciplines such as change management, systems theory, journalism, and marketing.

Many volumes have been written to help us improve our self-talk, our mindset, so that we can show up effectively and make a difference. But there is a sizable hole in the literature. (And anyway, who wants to read dry old literature?)

The gap is this: none of these books speak directly to you and I as social impact communicators. Whereas other communication professionals necessarily focus first on conveying new information, educating, or raising awareness, you and I daily focus first on opening people's hearts to make room for changes in thinking and behavior. My view is that social impact communication as a discipline is an umbrella inclusive of all communicators who work to effect positive change at unprecedented scale and on issues far greater than themselves, such as climate change or racial equity. You might be a business executive, or the leader of a nonprofit, or the director of a government agency. You could be a writer, an editor, a marketer, a journalist, a broadcaster, a data analyst, a politician, or a public relations professional. Each of these and many more can be social impact communicators with the proper framework. I propose to share just such a framework in this book.

Communication anchors each of these roles. Society needs them. (Don't laugh. I see you over there in the corner. If you can't say anything nice, don't say anything at all. Or so I tell my four children on particularly

INTRODUCTION

sassy days.) What distinguishes you as a social impact communicator, though, is that you do this all the time. Your personal values and the mission of your organization are focused on the big picture. You creatively pursue new projects and programs, products and services, with that big picture in mind 24/7. You experiment and build new communication approaches that have never been tried before.

This is the joy (and occasional pain) of a social impact communicator. And together, you and I are going to figure out the best strategies for effectively communicating and leading to make those changes we dream about a reality.

When I think about social impact communication, I like to imagine a sheet of paper with two columns and a line down the middle. On the left, I'd list "What social impact communication is," and on the right, I'd list "What social impact communication is not."

Table 1. What social impact communication is and is not

Social impact communication is…	Social impact communication is not…
A new communication discipline worthy of study	Conventional communications
A connection between your organization's value proposition and the values of your customers and partners	Activism or woke capitalism or whatever pejorative is in vogue
An aspirational discipline focused on achieving multigenerational change starting now	A fad that's going away
A blended discipline that combines language and leadership	Greenwashing or green hushing

Let's tackle the left-hand side of the list first by studying what social impact communication means. I'm going to give you my definition. You are free to disagree or add your own nuance. We are simply setting the stage.

INTRODUCTION

Social impact communication is a new communication discipline worthy of study, though it draws heavily on existing change theory and communication disciplines

You and I can benefit from a framework for social impact communication because we have come to the point in society that entire careers, departments, and divisions are being built around the social impact work I have described—the very work you do every day. This includes sustainability, climate change, equity, inclusion, and so on. Just as people in the past could specialize in architecture or computer programming or pharmacy, people today can specialize in topics whose core emphasis is social impact. This is distinct from building a product or shipping a service.

As a journalism school graduate student, I trained in convergence journalism. Convergence meant the coming together of newspapers, radios, TV, and the Internet for new, multimedia types of storytelling. I needed to be able to use these platforms to tell compelling stories, to secure and hold a job in the media. Today, this interdisciplinary communication is standard fare. Back then, it was revolutionary.

Consequently, I was as pleased as punch that I could manhandle a giant camera that weighed more than myself. I could sit in a recording booth and capture my voice for the radio. It changed my worldview. Up to that point, I had always assumed my face and voice were custom designed for print only.

One day in the future, social impact communication will be like this. Everyone will do it at some level, and there will be well-established groups of people who claim it as their specialty. It will strike everyone as, "Well, of course this exists. Of course we see why it matters."

xxiii

INTRODUCTION

But not always today. Today, the concept of social impact communication gets hearty approval, or mild applause, or looks of confusion. If it doesn't immediately contribute to the bottom line of your organization, good luck getting people to pay attention.

But you and I, we are going to change that. And we will all be better for it.

Social impact communication is a connection between your organization's value proposition and the values of your customers and partners

Even the most sophisticated, data-driven marketing that draws on people's umpteen zillion data points, biometric scans, and forecasts of future behavior hinges on a fundamental premise: People can be reduced to a number, and if you pull certain levers, you will increase your odds of an intended end result. This could be persuading someone to make a purchase or click a button or join a cause or make a donation. There is nothing wrong with opening people's minds to the possibilities around them—to the choices they could make to improve their lives. This isn't manipulation when applied ethically. There are certainly guardrails a person would want to follow to avoid twisting its customers' beliefs and bending them to their will.

But fundamentally, what's often at stake is a product or service or position. Do this because it will make your life better, and if it serves my organization, all the better. My bottom line will grow, more people will want to invest in my business, shareholders will be happy, and so on.

Happy capitalism aside, social impact communication is first about linking your organization's values to those of your audience. Your organization might be a nonprofit, or an association, or a successful local business, or a private global firm, or even a government agency. Social impact communication is agnostic in terms of the kind of organization delivering it so long as it cuts to the quick of the audiences' heart. Your audience might be a mom of two in need of ingredients for dinner or a single man in his 60s working on a home-improvement project. Social impact communication doesn't concern itself with market segments or target audiences but rather with individuals as something more: human beings with value beyond the power of their wallet.

Social impact communicators desire relationships over reaction. Certainly, social impact communication can complement an organization's marketing strategy, or PR activities, or corporate communications memos. But social impact communication is more. It is a message from the heart of an organization to the heart of the individual. It aspires to tell the truth and have that truth understood, if not also embraced, by the hearer.

Social impact communication is an aspirational discipline focused on achieving multigenerational change starting now

Another factor that sets apart social impact communication from other types of communication activity is its emphasis on the future. It is a vastly different future than we have today. In general, most of the content you and I consume today is designed to help make our current existence informed, improved, and impactful. We generally don't watch movie previews for a film due out in 100 years. We view previews because we want to go to the theater this weekend with our children, or to turn on the TV from the comfort of our own basements and watch it via our preferred streaming service.

Or imagine a new product for your kitchen or workshop or yard. "You won't believe the way this helps you," the ad might say, "and in 2392, you'll see it for yourself." Such a product would generate little more than laughter and cries of derision. For what good is a product coming onto the market in 300 years? I will not be around, nor will my children and grandchildren.

INTRODUCTION

You might as well tell me what it will be like to visit Pluto en route to the next galaxy over. We will all be long gone from fair Earth before that happens, unless you have access to some type of fearful new elixir. (I would love to discuss this elixir if you have it. Name your price!)

But I digress—for we are talking about things with more lasting value beyond elixirs.

What distinguishes social impact communication is that the content of the message, the change desired, the issues discussed, can start to be realized now. But it will ultimately yield exponentially greater benefits to future generations. If we begin to address a changing climate now, and stick with it, the consequences of cleaner air, more manageable weather events, and so on will be profound, based on what many scientists tell us. On the other hand, failure to act now could result in a deeply unpleasant future. This is especially true for those most vulnerable and at risk and without access to all of the energy and amenities of our western, US-oriented culture.

Social impact communication builds common understanding and cultivates shared values. These are issues all of us must solve together. In that respect, it is the opposite of marketing or journalism. Marketing appeals to specific segments who need to solve a specific problem. Journalism democratizes knowledge yet often appeals in practice to a specific subset of citizens or business people who value information for decision-making purposes. Social impact communication in its ideal form should offer something for everyone. It is broad and vast and yet deals with issues that all of us must face, sooner or later—if not us personally, then certainly those who come after us.

Social impact communication is a moral calling of the highest order that draws on the best of journalism, marketing, and other communication disciplines. And we don't have to agree on all the specifics to acknowledge that change in how we communicate is necessary if we want a happier outcome for everyone.

Social impact communication is a blended discipline that combines language and leadership

If you were a speechwriter for the president, you would think very carefully—at least we can hope—about the content of your message. You would be cautious to convey precisely what you meant without disclosing anything top secret or harmful that could jeopardize people's lives. (Again, assume we are in a vacuum—I know the real world is much more complicated, even for presidents.) You would take care to spend time with your speechwriting team poring over the language and ensuring it conveyed what you meant. You would ensure your "broccoli" wasn't meant to say "*E. coli*" instead. And then you would get up to the lectern and deliver your remarks with a tone and inflection that captured attention and conveyed meaning. You would choose the backdrop carefully rather than picking any old park or street corner or business for your message. The scenery, the words, the tone—all would convey a precise message.

Social impact communication brings a similar layer of nuance that might be unfamiliar or downright unnecessary in other disciplines. Many companies have dedicated leaders who focus only on internal communications. Others have folks focused exclusively on marketing—how your organization appears to the outside world. Social impact communication cuts through each of these with butter-knife precision. It doesn't seek to disrupt things. Rather, it seeks to infuse each type of communication discipline with the purpose and warmth of something great.

Social impact communication shows up in many places, as a result. It appears in annual reports; environmental, social, and governance (ESG) documents; or sustainability narratives. It crops up in investor briefings. It presents itself in press conferences with the media. It can even infuse your product marketing, packaging, and website copy.

INTRODUCTION

For a message to successfully run the race from a communicator's mind through the internal workings of an organization and out into the world, it must first be batted about by people within your team. This means social impact communicators must often persuade their colleagues that this type of storytelling is worthy of attention and focus. You might be tasked with making the case that your constituents are thinking about social impact issues and that your organization must address them. People seek meaning. People change their buying behavior to support brands that address issues of multigenerational significance. As Glow, a NielsenIQ partner, noted in a 2023 report on US consumers' food and grocery preferences, half of consumers report changing brands based on perceived ESG performance.[1]

In this way, social impact communication rejects silos and instead offers something beyond words: leadership. Highly effective social impact communicators are leaders who must first draw others in their organization to themselves. Once rapport and shared understanding are achieved, there must be a strategy for disseminating this activity through the organization. Eventually, it will spill outward on purpose and, when applied properly, soak into the minds and hearts of those you are trying to reach and engage.

It takes time, patience, practice, learning, and adjustments. It sometimes requires mistakes and forgiveness and trying again. These traits are the traits of leaders—leaders whose background is in social impact communication.

---

[1] "2023 US Brand Sustainability Benchmark Report: Food & Grocery Industry." Glow, a NielsenIQ partner. 2023. https://campaign.glowfeed.com/srs_foodgrocery_us

INTRODUCTION

Social impact communication is not conventional communication, though they draw on a common technical skill set

We have tackled the left-hand side of my imaginary paper (see Table 1). Now, let's turn our attention to the right-hand side of the page. Here, we find another category: what social impact communication is *not*. There are plenty of people who would say that social impact communication is simply a dolled-up version of things we already know well and practice, and that is partly true. They share a common technical skill set—writing, editing, storytelling, and so on. Why invest time, money, and attention in our organizations on something that is perfectly familiar? And on a darker note, why invest in something that seems dubious, controversial, or subject to lawsuits? If we ignore social impact communication or treat it as banal, surely it will go away and leave us alone.

Only it will not. The future world will rely on social impact communicators to shape our thinking and inform our actions. This unique style of communication will cultivate relationships and build shared understanding. The question is whether your organization will be prepared to take up the mantle of leadership.

You don't have to take my word for it. Allow me to illustrate why this is the case.

Sadly, newspapers continue to close at a rapid rate. Meanwhile, more and more people are getting information from many different channels, which seem to rise to prominence and sometimes fade as quickly as they arrive in our consciousness. As I am writing this, Facebook and X (formerly known as Twitter) face questions about whether they are proponents or enemies of free speech.

Meanwhile, long-form reading platforms such as Substack are giving writers and readers the chance to connect with minimal filters. Extended reality (XR) technologies are bringing virtual reality and real life together, enabling us to experience the world in new and immersive ways. I don't know what platforms will be popular by the time you read this, but it doesn't matter much. The point is this: The way we tell stories is changing, and so is the delivery vehicle. Yet the power of social impact storytelling will remain constant.

Increasingly, you will have more independence and autonomy to tell compelling stories. They will not necessarily be filtered as much or as controversially as they are today. This gives you freedom to experiment, try new things, and work with legacy communication skills and trusted media platforms without being bound to them.

As with conventional communication, truth-telling remains essential in this new mode of communication. Accuracy and authenticity are everything, especially in an era when artificial intelligence can invent stories, audio, and video from scratch. Social impact communication builds trust because it demonstrates the potential for good in the world and shows how it can actually be achieved. It runs counter to the negative content ecosystem that swirls around us.

Social impact communication is not activism or woke capitalism or whatever pejorative is in vogue

For those who are inherently skeptical of social impact communication, it might feel as though it is akin to activism. From this vantage point, it might appear as though organizations pick a cause, cling to it like mad, and loudly proclaim its virtues online and on street corners (which, by the way, is extremely unfair to generations of peaceful protesters, change-makers, and rabble-rousers, but I digress).

Social impact communication often gets billed as dressed-up ideology. The thing about social impact communication, though, is that it isn't trying to influence legislation or financial decisions or to bend the will of the people. Instead, it aims to illustrate how an organization's mission and impact align with the personal mission and desired impact of the people with whom it comes into contact. Social impact communication reveals rather than recommends. It opens eyes rather than controversies.

Some people have accused organizations focused on social impact issues of woke capitalism. The idea is that a company or a nonprofit can funnel its spending into activities that politically left-minded people care about, while all other activities and investors are left in the cold.

This one has always puzzled me. It seems to me that prioritizing the interests of customers, regardless of their political persuasion, is simply good business. Not at the expense of an organization's values, of course. But there are a lot of things that can make a business better: resilience in the face of environmental changes and severe weather. Greater inclusion of people from diverse backgrounds whose perspectives and experiences add breadth and depth to a company's bench.

Woke capitalism has been used to critique investment firms whose funds include companies that embrace ESG principles. Something more challenging is at work, though: the broad brush of "woke" to any activity that makes people feel as though companies have traded their values for a narrow-minded ideology.

The right way to think about social impact communication is as a discipline for bringing people and organizations together around common values. We just might be describing those values in different ways.

It's time to take off the eyeglasses of politics and instead focus on those things that are right and true as human beings.

Social impact communication is not a fad that's going away

You might think social impact communication will have its day in the sun and then crawl back into bed. Even though some data do show that younger generations still prioritize classic needs—such as convenience, affordability, and traditional vocations[2]—interest in environmental and societal issues remains strong. For example, one-third of Millennials and Gen Zers report "addressing climate change is my top concern," according to Pew Research Center.[3] And even if these attitudes and actions eventually fade, it's hard to imagine the fundamentals changing so significantly that they will wane and blink out altogether. Going where your customers are seems prudent.

Spend time thinking about how social impact issues affect the daily lives of your customers and constituents. Make a point of learning and understanding them better. Adapt your outreach and messaging so it's clear how your organization is contributing.

This isn't a call to compromise. Rather, it's an invitation to learn more about your customers and stakeholders. It's a chance to identify their priorities as they relate to the kinds of products, services, or projects you provide.

Line up your organization's values alongside these learnings. What do you see? I bet you'll find areas of common ground that can be woven into your social impact communication strategy. I'll show you how throughout the chapters to follow.

Social impact communication is not greenwashing or green hushing

Some organizations—fearful of how others will perceive their investment in social impact issues—silence themselves and choose not to speak about these activities. Fast Company labeled this strategy as "green hushing."[4]

---

[2] "Axios + Generation Lab Youth Poll Career Aspirations." January 2023. https://pdfhost.io/v/QI4r4sqG4_Axios_Career_Survey_Generation_Lab

[3] "Gen Z, Millennials Stand Out for Climate Change Activism, Social Media Engagement With Issue." Tyson et al. May 26, 2021. www.pewresearch.org/science/2021/05/26/gen-z-millennials-stand-out-for-climate-change-activism-social-media-engagement-with-issue/

[4] "What is 'green hushing'? The new negative sustainability trend, explained." Talib Visram. March 10, 2023. www.fastcompany.com/90858144/what-is-green-hushing-the-new-negative-sustainability-trend-explained

Better to act behind the scenes, the thinking goes, than in front of a judgmental audience. Meanwhile, another article the previous year in the same publication reported 68% of executives surveyed saying their company greenwashes, embellishing the truth about its sustainability activities.[5]

Social impact communication is neither something to hide in a back closet for fear of the angry mob nor a license to make up stories about your organization's virtues. That makes this discipline particularly challenging to navigate. After all, truth and authenticity in public sound scary. But I assure you it can be done, and it starts by getting clear on your own values, the good you do in the world, and the opportunities you have to grow and improve.

Too many brands err on the side of hubris or on the side of mealy-mouthed mediocrity. You can do better. This book will explain how.

Where we are headed: A preview of the seven secrets of highly effective social impact communicators

Now that we have established some guardrails, I want to give you a teaser for the rest of this book. Our goal is to help you embrace the tremendous potential of social impact communication, personally and professionally. When you can master this discipline, you can bring your customers and other audiences into a relationship with you in a way that builds lasting collaboration, trust, and impact. You will actually get more real things done versus talking about what those real things might be.

---

[5] "68% of U.S. execs admit their companies are guilty of greenwashing." Adele Peters. April 13, 2022. www.fastcompany.com/90740501/68-of-u-s-execs-admit-their-companies-are-guilty-of-greenwashing

To do this, I will share with you the seven secrets I have observed skilled social impact communicators implementing to make changes in the world and in their organizations.

Secret #1: Highly effective social impact communicators ... care both about the words and the mission

They get clear first on what they are doing and why. Then, they use their gift of story to bring others into community, conversation, and shared understanding.

Secret #2: Highly effective social impact communicators ... are astute translators inside and outside of their organizations

They use their unique position and expertise in the organization to connect dots internally and externally. The best of the best build a community of respect and shared commitment to the mission.

Secret #3: Highly effective social impact communicators ... leverage the strength of personal and organizational values to tell compelling stories

They know why they show up for work every day and apply those first principles to their craft. They feel called and drawn to be a part of this journey. Social impact communication unlocks the soul of their mission, which in turn benefits the organization and their audiences.

Secret #4: Highly effective social impact communicators ... embrace the renewable fuel of teamwork

They deeply value and nurture business relationships, knowing social impact communication is a big job far more than one person can handle. In this way, social impact communication is not a skill to be practiced but a leadership discipline to apply and help others.

Secret #5: Highly effective social impact communicators ... reframe every setback as the crest of a hill

They recognize the potential of social impact work to be isolating and discouraging. Rather than giving into hopelessness, they cultivate a resilient mindset that helps them view setbacks for what they really are: the crest of a hill before the next big breakthrough or positive outcome.

Secret #6: Highly effective social impact communicators ... cede perfection to the messy reality of change-making

They don't get bogged down in getting everything right or walking on eggshells. They practice planning, clarity, and persistence. They recognize they are charting paths no one has laid down before. This brings a certain amount of fear. It is overcomeable through courage and personal growth.

INTRODUCTION

Secret #7: Highly effective social impact communicators … build personal and professional legacies that outlive them and their careers

They fully believe they are part of something great and that its ripple effects will be felt for generations to come if they adopt the right habits. They think seriously about what they say and how they say it, and embrace those stories with confidence, because of their potential to make the world a more welcoming and equitable place.

So … how do I explain what I do once I've gotten clarity on how to do it well?

Throughout these pages, I'll share the insights and experiences I've gleaned along the way while growing as a social impact communicator and executive. This is the book I wish I'd had when I began working on climate change and racial equity. Your mission might be completely unrelated. That's OK. The principles I share here will still apply.

Along the way, I'll introduce you to a few of the many people doing incredible things in social impact communication. I want you to see how they came to their mindset of opportunity.

Before we move into the thick of things, let me tie a bow on the ballet story I introduced at the beginning of this chapter.

After I botched my explanation of what I do with my fellow daughter-dad, I spun in circles trying to figure out an elegant way to describe my profession.

What I realized is that social impact communicators ought to have the freedom to articulate what they do without being boxed in. After all, this space is big enough for diverse approaches and perspectives. But if you are looking for some specific coaching, I would encourage you to focus on what people think and feel after encountering your work as a social impact communicator. For example, you might tell a friend or family member:

- I tell stories that change society, one voice at a time.

- The content I create for my brand focuses first on building relationships and mindset bridges with thoughts and ideas, then on the products and/or services and/or projects we offer.

- I focus on capturing and sharing wisdom versus mystical woo-woo that can't be defined or practiced. Social impact communication is tangible and about tackling what we can see and hear around us, not a spiritual discipline or an emotional exercise, as important as those things are. We make a measurable impression on the world that starts with words and extends to actions.

In the end, what distinguishes you, as a social impact communicator, from other writers, editors, and creatives is your keen understanding of what's at stake—and the license you have to translate those stakes into language that speaks to your customers' hearts as much as to their heads. At the end of each chapter, you'll find several prompts. These questions will help you dive deeper and find more clarity on your own unique vantage point about social impact communication. I encourage you to stop, take time to journal or jot down some notes about the questions, and reference them again as you go through this book.

If you still aren't comfortable explaining what you do to others, bury your nose in this volume and I assure you, you'll have greater confidence by the time we're through together.

INTRODUCTION

Ready to get started? Let's begin with Secret #1: the ever-important role of a big, exciting, audacious mission in shaping who you become as a social impact communicator.

Key Questions

- To what degree do your personal values and professional mission align?
- What might be the first three steps you could take to better align your values and mission at work?
- How would you describe what you do to a friend?
- What are we doing right as social impact communicators? What's the No. 1 area for improvement, in your view?
- Where should the discipline of social impact communication go next to serve as many people as possible?

CHAPTER 1

Secret #1: Highly effective social impact communicators ... care both about the words and the mission

I fell in love with my own social impact mission long before I ever set foot in an office. It happened out on the farm.

My maternal grandfather, James King, lived as an enthusiastic naturalist. Perhaps it came naturally after spending years at the Avco manufacturing plant in Nashville working indoors on a very specific tailpiece of the C-130 aircraft.

He and my mamaw, Ann, bought a small farm of several dozen acres up the road from his parents. It proved a dream come true. Their three children, and later their nine grandchildren and many great-grandchildren, made wonderful memories there.

CHAPTER 1   SECRET #1: HIGHLY EFFECTIVE SOCIAL IMPACT COMMUNICATORS ... CARE BOTH ABOUT THE WORDS AND THE MISSION

Both watched the seasons pass gently on their farm, and they ate hundreds of home-cooked country meals in their kitchen, which could be stifling in the summer humidity of Tennessee. Now, both are buried on a hill in an old cemetery that overlooks the property.

During visits, Grandpa took us around the property to explore all the things he'd been doing—and all the insights he'd gleaned. We examined flowers he'd gently placed into planters to welcome the spring. We went on wagon rides behind his blue Ford tractor through the fields and observed deer running through the glades and woods. He pointed out where he'd one day own Boer goats, though the dream never materialized outside of his imagination.

To beat the heat, we'd head indoors into their farm home with its funhouse floors that never sat quite straight and its multicolored carpet and rugs added over the decades. Some rooms dated at least to the 1800s. Together, we'd examine big books with photographs from natural places. God's creation held his mind captive and fed his worldview with a steady stream of beauty and wonder. He admired leaders such as Theodore Roosevelt, whose investments helped conserve millions of acres of natural spaces.

When I wasn't visiting my grandparents with my family, my parents, Norman and Anita, took us across the country to visit national parks of all kinds. We traveled past the Arches of Utah and the majestic grandeur of the Rocky Mountains. Back then, you didn't need a pass or a walking stick to elbow past the throngs of eager tourists. You simply needed a decision to hit the road and the spirit of adventure.

As I grew up, I got active in nature-focused activities. My junior high, Westview Middle School, is located along the Front Range of Colorado. We had a wetlands area behind the building. I participated in a club that cleaned up trash and generally celebrated this quaint and quiet oasis where red-winged blackbirds trilled their lullabies and insects orchestrated a never-ending symphony against the blue Rocky Mountains.

CHAPTER 1   SECRET #1: HIGHLY EFFECTIVE SOCIAL IMPACT COMMUNICATORS ... CARE BOTH ABOUT THE WORDS AND THE MISSION

As a college student and early professional, I found myself drawn away from the field and farm and toward the big city and even bigger mastheads across the newspapers where I wanted to work. I interned with the *Detroit Free Press*, worked for them remotely for several years, and went on to run a small newsroom in Boonville along the Missouri River.

But within a few years, I was right back in rural America covering agriculture for a revered B2B company. I spent the next decade leaning into this incredible industry, working with dozens of food and agriculture organizations, and observing what great social impact communicators do best.

It all began in my past on the farm and in wild spaces, tromping around with waders in the wetlands.

Define the mission and why it matters to you

A keen understanding of the mission and why it matters to you is the first secret of every social impact communicator. The mission is at the heart of what you do each day as a professional. It also ends up shaping you.

You don't need to worry about having every detail of that mission worked out. In fact, many professional communicators I know first found an organization that fit them exceptionally. Then, they fell into the work—and fell in love with the mission. Whether you know precisely what mission you hope to work toward, or whether you uncover a passion for that mission with time in your organization, there is no wrong way to go about it. Let the journey be your guide.

Do you want to be a great social impact communicator? Would you like to improve and grow at your craft? It starts by getting clear about what your mission actually is. Once you define it, the communication skills you cultivate can be applied to any social impact mission you might pursue in the future, no matter your title or industry.

CHAPTER 1 SECRET #1: HIGHLY EFFECTIVE SOCIAL IMPACT COMMUNICATORS ... CARE BOTH ABOUT THE WORDS AND THE MISSION

I suggest starting the mission-defining process by interviewing yourself. Maybe do this in a room with a door to avoid stares and raised eyebrows. Jot down these questions along with some initial observations about how you might answer them:

- If you had to trace your own narrative arc—the scenes and experiences that got you deep into the mission of social impact work—what would it sound like? What images would play back in your mind? How would you describe it to a friend?

- What piece of the mission makes you get up every morning and say, "I know why I'm here. I know what I'm supposed to be doing."

- When you think about the mission of your organization, which pieces stir your soul the most? Which pieces do you immediately want to share with someone you care about?

- If you had to describe the mission using the most descriptive words possible, what would you say? How would you describe it to a kindergartener? To a PhD-holding professor?

- What gives you confidence the mission is achievable? What keeps you going?

These kinds of questions will help you get a grasp of the crux of what you are doing. They are important because they will take you a layer deeper, into the heart and soul of your mission.

For many social impact communicators, the "what" defines their everyday life. For example, your "what" might sound like, "We are developing products that can sequester carbon and mitigate the risk of global warming." (Of course, if anyone had a single product to do this, we'd all be using it and making great strides. If this describes you, please contact me so we can get this out to the market quickly!)

The "what" is essential, but it is also too basic for our purposes. As you reflect on your personal and professional mission, ask a deeper question: What is the "so that" your mission makes possible?

The question of "so that" pushes us to think more deeply about the impact of our work. This is especially important in social impact efforts because, as we will discuss toward the end of this book, they are designed (or at least ought to be, in my mind) for multiple generations. You do not produce widgets that are placed on shelves today and discarded tomorrow. You are sowing the seeds of ideas and innovations that will benefit society for years and years to come. As such, it is important to think about how the messages and communications you deliver over a long time horizon could shape society. This is the beauty of the "so that" question.

Framing your mission in the form of a statement can help clarify your "so that." For example:

- Our products sequester carbon and mitigate the risk of global warming *so that* future generations avoid severe heat and other consequences of a warming atmosphere and enjoy happy, healthy lives.

- Our services keep water clean *so that* historically underserved communities avoid the many health risks of dirty water and enjoy the same access to fresh water that every human being deserves.

- Our project connects farmers with the information and technical support they need to integrate regenerative practices into their businesses. This is *so that* they can reap the full financial, environmental, and social benefits of practices that boost soil health.

CHAPTER 1   SECRET #1: HIGHLY EFFECTIVE SOCIAL IMPACT COMMUNICATORS ... CARE BOTH ABOUT THE WORDS AND THE MISSION

As you consider your own work, you will discover all kinds of potential positive outcomes inside your mission. These insights will serve as your anchor. It's particularly necessary that you anchor your work this way. All of us have experienced the gale-force winds of the modern workplace, which can experience rapid change, fire drills, and sprints from one activity to the next. A deeply anchored mission helps you remain focused and steady to do meaningful work.

This anchor is important for several other reasons, as well.

First, it gives your social impact communication deeper purpose. Whether you are preparing a speech for an executive on ESG issues, writing an annual report, or developing a campaign for social media, your mission informs how you approach the work. It determines how you craft stories about your organization's social impact activities.

Second, your mission serves as true north when things get messy (more about working through the mess in Chapter 6). When life's thunderstorms appear on the horizon, and you can barely see a foot in front of your face, the mission and the feelings it evokes inside of you and your team will pull you forward. This is far better than the alternative, which is trying to force yourself through the storm and into a better mindset in the absence of a deep calling. An anchoring mission creates the right conditions for a mindset of resilience, optimism, and social impact effectiveness.

Finally, your mission will help you decide which words and language you'll need to describe your social impact work effectively. Mission helps you maintain or even accelerate the momentum of your organization.

A word about technical skill

Because you picked up a book for communication professionals, I'm going to assume you know a thing or two about writing, editing, and influencing others with words. But I'd be remiss if I glossed over just how important those communication fundamentals are to your social impact mission.

CHAPTER 1   SECRET #1: HIGHLY EFFECTIVE SOCIAL IMPACT COMMUNICATORS ... CARE BOTH ABOUT THE WORDS AND THE MISSION

Once as a young journalist, my editor sent me out on assignment to cover a sensitive story. People in our community were remembering a police officer who had been killed on duty under tragic circumstances on the one-year anniversary of the event. I attended the memorial, headed back to my computer, and put together a piece that I felt reflected the gravity and significance of the event.

Only it didn't. My editor quickly called my attention to the fact my story needed work. Despite the awkwardness of the situation, we worked together and crafted a more nuanced, detailed, and appropriate recounting—the first rough draft of history, as they sometimes say.

The same is true for your social impact communication. You can have the best of intentions and miss the mark—in your research, your planning, your execution. To be your best, practice your craft of storytelling in whatever mediums you use—online, video, print, and so on. Get regular feedback from people you trust to give you sound communication advice, people who've done this work for a long time. Read books and take continuing education to learn and improve.

A mentor once told me, "A coach without a coach is a fraud." In a similar vein, whether you use those technical skills exclusively on your own projects—or more likely, to lead and coach other communicators delivering your organization's social impact work—you must grow yourself technically in order to see the outcomes you desire.

Harness the power of purpose

Confidence is a terribly misunderstood character trait. It's not innate, at least as far as I know. Instead, it must be earned. And the only way you earn it is to practice it.

CHAPTER 1   SECRET #1: HIGHLY EFFECTIVE SOCIAL IMPACT COMMUNICATORS ... CARE BOTH ABOUT THE WORDS AND THE MISSION

In the early days of my social impact wading, I can vividly recall attending the enormous Sustainable Brands conferences. I was mesmerized by how people spoke. The kinds of conversations they had. The caliber of executive speakers who presented. The sense of community amazed me.

I had little reason to be confident at the time, as a relative newcomer to the social impact community. Most of the professionals I encountered didn't know me from Adam. I had far more questions than answers.

Yet people agreed to meet with me. A conversation with an intrepid if amateur business person wouldn't deter their mission, evidently.

I met with a European restaurateur who was among the first in the world to put climate impact labels on a menu. The team at a major food and beverage company agreed to spend time answering my questions.

I familiarized myself with the language these leaders spoke. I observed the issues that mattered to them. I sat in on breakout sessions where people had the opportunity to ask questions and dive deeper. The conversations were mostly foreign to me but made me aware I needed to pay attention. Much of my work involved informing and engaging farmers and ranchers in those days. They weren't sitting in the room alongside me. I had a responsibility to share with them what I'd heard. The social impact goals of food and agriculture companies would eventually impact their businesses in rural America.

In this sense, confidence is more of a habit than a skill. Repeated exposure to unfamiliar surroundings will eventually make you more comfortable in the arena. As a social impact communicator, you might find yourself in these kinds of new situations routinely. You might be trying to explain a fine point of social impact to a colleague—dare I say, an executive. Or you might put together a marketing campaign for a B2B or a consumer audience. Even the best data and research can't always predict with certainty how a social impact message will land with an audience.

CHAPTER 1   SECRET #1: HIGHLY EFFECTIVE SOCIAL IMPACT COMMUNICATORS ... CARE BOTH ABOUT THE WORDS AND THE MISSION

But because you have cultivated the discipline of confidence, you will move forward, applying the best knowledge you have and recognizing that the mission makes the discomfort worth it. You'll learn something through this process. Your outreach will be more effective in the future because of how you've applied it.

It's also important to pair your confidence with a sense of belonging. For years, I have struggled with my own inner game of self-talk. Jon Acuff's book *Soundtracks* is brilliant, and I highly recommend it for freeing you from the negative loops in your head that discourage you and suggest you're never going to make it.

The story I told myself again and again was that I was an oddball in a sea of people who belonged. What did a person from Mexico, Missouri, (yes, it's a real place!) have to offer a bunch of people from the city who clearly were the hippest, most in tune, and most strategic leaders out there?

This feeling was especially acute at conferences and social gatherings. I had to muster the courage to say something kind and intelligent. Or at least not completely idiotic. Carrying a press pass at many of these events helped break the ice because, of course, anyone who looks like free PR is a friend. (I jest.)

The respect and sincerity of the people I met convinced me the social impact community is big enough for all of us. It's big enough for you and your mission, too.

Curiosity drives you to keep discovering new facets of the mission

One of the most rewarding aspects of being a social impact communicator is the need to stay glued into current events and trends. I've never been much of a pop culture nerd, or an entertainment nerd, or a sports nerd.

CHAPTER 1   SECRET #1: HIGHLY EFFECTIVE SOCIAL IMPACT COMMUNICATORS ... CARE BOTH ABOUT THE WORDS AND THE MISSION

But social impact nerd? Oh baby.

I approach work with my clients with the zest of a kid in a candy shop. Or, more on brand for me, a kid in a library. The journalist in me shoves everyone else in my mind to the backseat. I have a thousand questions and all the time in the world.

Rather than jumping straight into questions, I do research first. I spend time learning about leaders and team members at an organization. I study how they describe their social impact mission on their website, in annual reports and whitepapers, and in online videos.

These insights prepare me for intelligent conversation. You can use this approach when preparing to take on a new social impact assignment, too.

I call it the three-part Social Impact 101 Assessment.

Part 1: Commit nothing to memory save impressions and a handful of key insights

As a social impact communicator, your role is to survey the landscape of a product, service, or program. People are depending on you to understand the social impact issue being solved, the people tasked with solving it, and the learnings being captured along the way. Consider how this particular issue or project strikes you at the heart level, not just its intellectual or material merits. Commit those feelings and emotions to memory: joy, healing, concern, and so on. Then, learn some basic facts, figures, or anecdotes based on what you've learned about this social impact effort from colleagues or independent research. This will allow you to properly translate the issues so others appreciate them and want to take action on them. (More on the secret superpower of translation in Chapter 2.)

CHAPTER 1   SECRET #1: HIGHLY EFFECTIVE SOCIAL IMPACT COMMUNICATORS ... CARE BOTH ABOUT THE WORDS AND THE MISSION

Part 2: Do your homework about that social impact issue

To be a social impact communicator is to be a conversationalist. The best conversations work in two directions. So if you want to lead a project, or design a communications campaign, or any other activities, you must learn as much as you can—and then share freely. You'll share with teammates and partners who are building communications efforts alongside you. And you'll weave those insights and perspectives into the very content and messages you create. Use the Internet. Scroll LinkedIn for expert perspectives. See how your social impact effort fits into the wider context of what's happening in your industry. See how other industries are solving for that specific social impact issue, too.

Part 3: Ask experts directly to fully understand the context

There will come a time in most social impact projects, often early on, when you need to move beyond the learning and into the doing. Through your study and research, you have now observed the landscape, met some of the key issues and people involved, and started to see how your effort fits into this context. That means it's now time to get this specific social impact communications effort underway. Schedule the meeting. Prepare questions based on what you've learned—and what gaps you're still trying to fill in. Conduct interviews with trusted experts over coffee, over Zoom, or in person.

Approach any social impact communications project with this type of wide-eyed curiosity and you're sure to learn. It's also far more enjoyable than alternative approaches, such as the following:

- **Panic:** How do I even begin to understand this complex topic so I can talk about it intelligently?

CHAPTER 1   SECRET #1: HIGHLY EFFECTIVE SOCIAL IMPACT COMMUNICATORS ... CARE BOTH ABOUT THE WORDS AND THE MISSION

- **Frustration:** Great, another bowl of verbal spaghetti I get to sort out and prepare for prime time.

- **Guilt:** If I get this wrong, we're all up a creek and I'm the one holding the paddle.

What could curiosity enable in your own organization's social impact mission? Here are some things you might discover when you apply curiosity about your mission:

- **More and better questions:** Curiosity improves your ability to look at your organization's services, products, or projects from every angle. How are things running now? Could there be a better way to talk about this effort? How are you measuring impact? Are there alternative angles you should pursue? What are the potential ways you could achieve these goals faster and more efficiently? What new goals could you set? Keep a running Word document or journal where you can jot down the questions you encounter. Use them as prompts for meeting with your team managing social impact communication. You'll be surprised at the exciting new paths you can pursue together when you brainstorm great questions to address.

- **Greater wonder and lower stress:** Social impact work often is painstaking because it's so new and because there are so few black-and-white answers. It can also face barriers such as funding and lack of clarity about how to measure social impact outcomes. Its newness can evoke unfamiliarity or skepticism. Hold onto curiosity for its replenishing capabilities. Be amazed at success stories you hear about how your organization's mission has helped improve environmental impact,

CHAPTER 1 SECRET #1: HIGHLY EFFECTIVE SOCIAL IMPACT COMMUNICATORS ... CARE BOTH ABOUT THE WORDS AND THE MISSION

serve under-resourced communities, or give people more choices. Dig deep with the scientists, marketers, or other team members in and outside of your organization who help implement your social impact mission. This space is wide and deep. Putting the mission into practice requires a team of diverse thinkers and doers. You can learn so much when you stop and consider all the ways your mission is evolving, growing, and making a difference.

- **More joy from the humanity of social impact work:** The human touch is one of my favorite parts of social impact work. Growing up near Boulder, Colorado, I spent a lot of time on Pearl Street Mall. This outdoor mall is famous for its entertainers, performers, and peaceful protesters. I'd listen to street musicians, hear people advocate for political causes, and observe how people very different from me engaged in the world. I absolutely loved it. When you bring curiosity to your mission first rather than harsh judgment, you see all the things other people can teach you. You also spot the talents and skills they can bring to advancing the mission. As a social impact communicator, you are called on to help ease internal processes and smooth other teamwork (more on that in Chapter 2). You're not just a mouthpiece for your organization. You're a conduit for the exchange of ideas, culture, and shared understanding within your organization. Get to know who people are—and why they are. What makes them tic? What lights up their eyes? Become the social impact communicator who gives people the space to be themselves, show up at work without apology, and do what they do best.

CHAPTER 1   SECRET #1: HIGHLY EFFECTIVE SOCIAL IMPACT COMMUNICATORS ... CARE BOTH ABOUT THE WORDS AND THE MISSION

Bryan Davis is the author of the acclaimed Christian children's fantasy book series, *Dragons In Our Midst*. I met him at a book signing and, as a newbie author, started asking questions. How did you land your first book deal? What was the process like?

He explained that he'd encountered more than 200 rejections by snail mail alone before a small publisher that wanted to expand its collection into his genre—dragons—took a chance on him. I told him how encouraging I found his story.

"You're glad I got rejected?" Davis replied in mock offense. We shared a laugh. My point to him—and to you, dear reader—is that knowing the struggles others encounter amid their mission can be encouraging. It shows us that our mission can in fact be successful if we keep at it, as hard as it can be. (And for the record, I'm thankful to the entire Apress team for taking a chance on this book idea well before I wrote these words!)

Curiosity will serve you well by giving you the courage and creative freedom to ask questions. You can imagine whole new worlds and maintain a resilient mindset on the mission. You might describe it differently tomorrow than you do today. Your focus might shift, and that might require updated talking points. But the heartbeat of the mission drives you forward. It inspires you to greater heights of learning and progress.

Know yourself best to be the best mission-bearer

In elementary school, I had no interest in gym class (which we called physical education, or P.E. for short). I didn't want to set foot on a kickball field. I had zero desire to climb the playground equipment at recess. (Other than escaping to the topmost turret of a slide, where I could read a good book). I preferred to keep learning and engaging my imagination.

CHAPTER 1 SECRET #1: HIGHLY EFFECTIVE SOCIAL IMPACT COMMUNICATORS ... CARE BOTH ABOUT THE WORDS AND THE MISSION

I'd park myself along the brick-lined walls of the school building, not too far from the cafeteria, and read. The teacher on duty would ask me, well, didn't I want to go play? And I'd say, "No, thank you. I'm reading," and go back to my book. Perhaps that explains why I'm now voluntarily clacking away at the keys.

As a child, you were probably cooler and more fun than I was. Yet I suspect we also would have found common cause because you've made it this far in this book.

You crave knowledge.

To a social impact communicator, learning is the currency of progress. It enables the mission to happen. The more you know, the more creative you can become in your storytelling. The more you study your limiting beliefs, your drivers, your team, your social impact progress, and your motivations, the better equipped you are to know which step to take next.

Learning first takes the form of becoming self-aware. The best social impact communicators I've encountered have a clear sense of who they are. They are able to find times to focus and times to rally their teams. They are deeply interested in the inner workings of everyone on the team. They are enthusiastic. They convene colleagues within and outside of their organization who are moving the ball down the court. (To use a sports analogy that never would have occurred to me in my bookish youth.)

Because I don't come from a farming background, I had to build my food supply chain vocabulary even further working as a social impact professional in food and agriculture.

Every new insight got labeled and shelved in my brain. I got a better sense of the issues clients prioritized and why. Trusted peers taught me the power of regular interaction with partner organizations to build rapport, build shared commitment to the social impact mission, and stay on track.

CHAPTER 1   SECRET #1: HIGHLY EFFECTIVE SOCIAL IMPACT COMMUNICATORS ... CARE BOTH ABOUT THE WORDS AND THE MISSION

They say that absence makes the heart grow fonder, but I say *accountability*—to yourself and to one another—is where the real magic happens. Social impact work thrives on community and conversation. It's in these environments that we learn, consider next steps, and make choices about how to keep after a goal and make progress.

Better to meet and have few updates to share than to avoid meeting and to lose track of one another's lives and sense of shared mission.

Always be learning. You won't regret it. It aids the mission.

Practical ways to put your social impact mission before the words you use

By now you might say to yourself, "Nate, you have clearly done some things in social impact. But I am not at all clear how I can use this in my own very different mission or industry. I don't live or work on a farm."

Well, that is where we are headed next. I am going to give you some very tangible things to think about. Remember, the journey we are on is one of building a richer and more expansive mindset. Master how you think about social impact communication. It will help you be much more prepared to handle anything on your team, with your clients, or any entrepreneurial ventures you pursue in the future.

Here are six things you can do right now to ensure you have the mission clearly in your line of sight. Trust me when I say that the words will follow. Whether you're writing copy for a billboard, preparing executive talking points for your CEO, or staging a conference, these focal points will serve you well.

CHAPTER 1   SECRET #1: HIGHLY EFFECTIVE SOCIAL IMPACT COMMUNICATORS ... CARE BOTH ABOUT THE WORDS AND THE MISSION

1. Understand what's at stake

The work of social impact has consequences beyond tomorrow's Wall Street (or Main Street) opening bell. You are not doing this work to command a paycheck without regard for the influence you're having on the world. Of course, getting paid is important, and I hope you are drawing a salary.

If you are running a startup and not yet taking a paycheck, hang in there. I admire you more than you know because I've started a business and recognize the discipline, faith, and fortitude it requires. Recognize what could happen if you choose not to act. Will wildlife lose access to critical habitat? Will whole communities of people miss out on opportunities that could have transformed their livelihoods for generations? Will future leaders fail to tap into a rich community of mentors?

Every social impact mission is unique, but all share one thing in common: without them, the world would be a darker and less hopeful place. Be the light, and go toward it.

2. Understand what's at risk

In his famous *Building a Story Brand*, author and business executive Donald Miller plots the arc of the classic story. The most compelling stories identify the hero and the sherpa who helps the hero on their mission, of course. But they also point out what success will look like if the hero succeeds. On the flip side, these stories clearly state the risks that loom large if the hero fails.

Borrowing this story arc is a brilliant approach to marketing. It's just as brilliant applied to social impact. No one wants to languish over the warming climate or persistent inequity. It's horribly sad and doesn't get us any closer to a solution.

CHAPTER 1   SECRET #1: HIGHLY EFFECTIVE SOCIAL IMPACT COMMUNICATORS ... CARE BOTH ABOUT THE WORDS AND THE MISSION

Yet, it's also important to be honest and open about why we're doing what we're doing. In many cases, that includes drawing attention to what we're working hard to avoid.

Turn the people who will benefit from your successful mission into heroes. Similarly, there might be other benefits that also can be cast in the role of hero. These might include our planet, the ecosystems you serve, or the communities whose lives will forever change for the better.

Remember: The journey is about *them*, not you. They are worth your effort so that the risks they face can be avoided. You as a social impact communicator show what's possible and what's avoidable.

3. Crave a brighter world with better opportunities

I'll never forget two vacations I vividly imagined and never experienced. They happened under very different circumstances. They aptly illustrate the principle of imagining a better world in which you will actually get to live.

The first vacation of imagination happened in my teenage years. My dad and mom have worked hard all their lives and are the absolute best parents anyone could ask for. So when they told us they had planned a trip to Disneyland in California, we were elated.

Then reality struck: My dad's job as a computer programmer vanished amid downsizing. My parents were open and honest with us. As much as they had dreamed of taking us on a special adventure, it wouldn't happen. I don't remember being crushed at all by the experience. We rallied around my dad and made it through, even though things would be different. We had imagined what it might be like at Disneyland, even though we never experienced it.

CHAPTER 1   SECRET #1: HIGHLY EFFECTIVE SOCIAL IMPACT COMMUNICATORS ... CARE BOTH ABOUT THE WORDS AND THE MISSION

The second vacation-that-wasn't slipped through my fingers as the coronavirus pandemic accelerated in early 2020. My wife and I had booked a Caribbean cruise to celebrate our ten-year wedding anniversary—two years after the fact. With four children in tow, luxury vacations for couples weren't exactly easy to secure.

(Incidentally, if you are a social impact entrepreneur looking for a project, trustworthy and extended-stay child care for families of 4+ children would be an excellent project. I will invest! Please contact me. Seriously. I am so desperate. Kidding! My children are wonderful.)

With each week that passed, new headlines emerged that suggested we'd be cutting it close on the cruise. Businesses began to cancel events. Countries sealed their borders.

Eventually, that fateful day arrived. Our cruise provider emailed us the bad news: the warm beaches, snorkeling sessions, and rainforest exploration wouldn't happen. Instead, we'd park ourselves at home and soak up the rays of quality Midwestern family time.

Julie and I had the cruise dream all ready. Our itineraries were booked and our suite aboard the ship reserved. But it only happened in our imaginations.

You have the potential to do one better than that, though. You can put your skills to work as a social impact communicator ***and move us all toward a brighter future that we might experience in our lifetimes***. I'll share toward the end of this book why you're actually setting the stage not just for us but for whole generations of future human beings. They can reap richly from the seeds you're planting today, too.

Imagine what's possible. Stretch the limits of your organization's mission. And then, foster with your words and actions the team and sense of community that will help make it possible. Social impact work can feel frustratingly slow at times. Learn to look for the signs you're making progress. Notice how you're feeling. Pay attention to your stress level. See how the level of excitement grows with each progressive win.

You are making traction on the mission. Keep at it.

CHAPTER 1   SECRET #1: HIGHLY EFFECTIVE SOCIAL IMPACT COMMUNICATORS ... CARE BOTH ABOUT THE WORDS AND THE MISSION

4. Feel compelled to bring others alongside you

Fellow University of Missouri graduate and famed executive David Novak, former CEO of Yum! Brands, has an incredible book called *Taking People With You*. I love that book for its approachability. Novak points out that if you want to build a great team and have tremendous influence as a communicator, you should start by showing people you care about them. Recognition and celebration of their accomplishments are crucial.

Social impact communicators who are laser focused on the mission never lose sight of what makes it a mission in the first place. The mission's success lies with the people who implement processes, practices, and disciplines that, when repeated and honed each day, lead to amazing results. I'll have much more to say about the renewable power of teamwork in Chapter 4.

"You'll never accomplish anything big," Novak writes, "if you try to do it alone."

You and your leadership team will know when you have the right team, when there's a person missing, and, as hard as it will be, when there is someone on the mission crew who isn't a fit. I didn't promise you that social impact communication—both a skill that can be honed and a leadership discipline—would be easy. Look back to the earlier lessons we discussed and apply those in your interactions with those you are bringing with you. What are you learning about your team?

Understand what's at stake if your team is successful. Will this group of people have what it takes to get to where you all want to go?

Recognize what's at risk. If you and your colleague who isn't a fit invest blood, sweat, and tears knowing full well it isn't a fit, will that get either of you any closer to the mission?

CHAPTER 1   SECRET #1: HIGHLY EFFECTIVE SOCIAL IMPACT COMMUNICATORS ... CARE BOTH ABOUT THE WORDS AND THE MISSION

Your commitment to the mission will require you to make tough choices. But if you are all in agreement that the mission matters, it will make those tough calls easier. You care more about the mission than about the words, though of course you should always take care with the words you use with your team and your partners.

Compassion and honest dialogue go a long way.

5. Fuse communication and leadership together

No social impact communicator worth their salt is simply a word processing wizard. They're also adept at working with people, taking instruction, making recommendations, asking astute questions, championing their mission internally and externally, and always looking ahead to the horizon for what's coming next.

In this way, social impact communication is as much about leadership as it is about sentence structure and grammatical errata. When you sign up to be a social impact communicator, you are signing up to be the person who deftly navigates some of the hardest, most vexing issues in the history of mankind. What a thrill!

Some people won't want that level of responsibility. That's OK. It isn't for everyone. The opportunities are great, and the risks of getting it wrong, or missing the mark, are enormous.

What has kept me going in my career in this field is the recognition that I'm hardly alone. There are so many talented, bright people in all kinds of industries working to solve these social impact challenges. And there are yet more bright young professionals joining our ranks who will take us to heights unknown.

It gives me such hope for my children and the professionals I've had the privilege to mentor to know that their passion for this work and their creativity are unparalleled. It charges every electric battery in my brain.

CHAPTER 1   SECRET #1: HIGHLY EFFECTIVE SOCIAL IMPACT COMMUNICATORS ... CARE BOTH ABOUT THE WORDS AND THE MISSION

6. Clarify your vision and talk about it

My dad tells the story of the time in his early childhood when he first got eyeglasses. He was mesmerized at how crisp everything looked around him. Every detail seemed sharper, and the colors seemed brighter. And best of all: He could see the chalkboard at school!

Or take flying. I love traveling by plane because I can see the world far better this way than on the ground. You can soar over a community and watch where the city ends and the rural landscape begins. The Earth appears as a series of blocks in a cosmic quilt dotted with circle-shaped trees and thin strips of fabric rivers. In the urban areas, strings of Christmas lights are actually cars traveling hurriedly to their final destination amid a blocky sea of Lego buildings. To me, these scenes will never get old. They are composed of endless variety and a sense of life and motion happening all the time, mostly out of our sight and mind.

When you are a social impact communicator, the vision of the future you see is radiant. You might as well be putting on new eyeglasses or traveling into the upper atmosphere in a plane to glimpse the world below. You have painted this picture in your mind a thousand times. You can hear what people will be saying about your accomplished social impact mission. You can feel the joy and blessing of achievement.

In some respects, social impact work has no true end point. Consider work to address climate change. It is wonderful to think there could come a time when all of us across the world reduce emissions, improve air quality, and mitigate the risk of a warming atmosphere. In that world, we would see the improvements to wild spaces, densely populated cities, and everywhere in between.

But once it happens—if it happens—what then? Will we simply stop the work and let things go back to the way they were? Of course not. There will be new data points and insights, new challenges to solve, more environmental issues to address together: water scarcity, soil health, and wildlife habitat are all areas in which I've worked. They will need help and protection in the future just as they do now.

Social impact communication is a discipline of constant remembrance and attention to the finer details. Yet we must not lose sight of the real possibility that we can make a difference. That it will be worth it. That the benefits will be expansive and inclusive. And that when we arrive, we will all be happier and healthier people.

Being a social impact communicator means staying focused enough to get today's work done while always keeping in your mind's eye that crystal clear tomorrow. See it for yourself, in all its Technicolor glory.

The mission reminds you social impact is achievable

Whether you work in cleantech or fintech, health or human resources, the restaurant industry or community building, mission is the anchor that grounds and directs your social impact communications.

Yet a mission does not sit on a pedestal for everyone to view plainly as in a museum gallery. It is buried in hearts and minds, waiting to be discovered and defined and used to make the world better and more vibrant.

That means a mission requires work. To understand it. To learn about the people behind it. To describe it and share it so it inspires and moves others to action.

When you focus first on your mission, and then on your words, you will reap these rewards—and potentially far greater ones than I've described here.

Imagine what's possible, share that bold vision with others, and then get to work by putting on your communications hat. Your mission is more beautiful than you can possibly dream.

Words are a tool to get someplace better. Your heart for the mission is the rudder that will take you there.

CHAPTER 1   SECRET #1: HIGHLY EFFECTIVE SOCIAL IMPACT COMMUNICATORS ... CARE BOTH ABOUT THE WORDS AND THE MISSION

Key Questions

- What mission gets you to show up for work every day ready to make a difference?

- What about the mission that makes you pumped?

- What difference do you want to see in the world? What changes do you want to make?

- What specifically will be the changes you personally create? How will you measure success?

- What will you do to celebrate those mission-driven accomplishments?

CHAPTER 2

Secret #2: Highly effective social impact communicators ... are astute translators inside and outside of their organizations

As the oldest of four children, peacemaker is a title I've proudly worn from my youth. I'm sure I didn't always succeed at it, but I had an innate desire to help people get along and appreciate one another.

I so prized this type of calm environment that my two brothers used it against me one day. Knowing I never wanted to get crosswise with my parents, they hatched a scheme with my dad—an eternally patient man— to pretend as though I'd really crossed a line.

I happened to be upstairs minding my own business one day. All of a sudden, my dad's normally calm voice boomed at me from the basement.

CHAPTER 2   SECRET #2: HIGHLY EFFECTIVE SOCIAL IMPACT COMMUNICATORS ...
              ARE ASTUTE TRANSLATORS INSIDE AND OUTSIDE OF THEIR ORGANIZATIONS

"Nathan," he said, "get down here right now!"

Mortified, I slunk down the stairs to discover my dad and brothers holding their stomachs, bent over in laughter. The ruse had worked.

It scared me at the time. Now, I think it's hilarious. I had misjudged the moment, not because I had failed in my role as a translator of my dad's intentions but because my brothers had taken that inbuilt desire and hacked it.

As a social impact communicator, the ability to walk between worlds, understand what's said and what's intended, and use that to develop meaningful social impact programs is essential. It's the second secret of how effective social impact communicators work. And it should help you avoid getting scolded by your boss or your dad—maybe both.

Navigate friction with the future in mind

In large part, translational skills are necessary because social impact projects and activities act as a magnet for tension. Some leaders in your organization might prioritize these projects above most everything else. Others won't necessarily see the business case for doing so, and they will object. Many might see and appreciate the mission yet approach it in different ways. Helping people arrive at a shared understanding of a problem, and the potential solutions, is a natural part of any social impact communicator's role.

It's important to get this right, internally and externally.

Many organizations implement real or imaginary silos that carve up their communications and make translation especially important. I suspect it's based mostly on tradition than on modern communication needs. For example, a lot of companies have a corporate communications team focused on relaying messages to employees inside an organization. Then, they have marketing and public relations teams for communicating

CHAPTER 2   SECRET #2: HIGHLY EFFECTIVE SOCIAL IMPACT COMMUNICATORS ... ARE ASTUTE TRANSLATORS INSIDE AND OUTSIDE OF THEIR ORGANIZATIONS

outside of the organization. Both are talented with words, yet both have different priorities and ways of talking about those priorities.

If more organizations developed a comprehensive social impact communication plan cutting across all of those disciplines, I suspect it could be more effective. It would draw on the strengths of each group. More importantly, it would create greater cohesion before organizations even began breathing a word about their environmental, social, and governance goals.

I've had the privilege of serving as a translator at many points in my career. At various times, I've communicated between journalists and sustainability professionals, between sustainability experts and agribusiness leaders, and between farmers and food executives.

Consequently, I became proficient at reading body language. I learned how to explain to leaders when guidelines provided to front-line colleagues weren't translating. I studied and tried out ways to work together more collaboratively.

Unless we aligned on the vision, the mission, and the "so that," we weren't going to get anywhere fast.

In this chapter, we'll dive deep to assess how you can become the most effective translational communicator. That's how a leader once described my ability to listen deeply and then collaborate to get two groups of people onto the same page.

I want to share a few things I've learned that might be helpful in your own social impact communication journey.

Then, I will illustrate the results you experience when you work adeptly as a social impact communicator.

CHAPTER 2   SECRET #2: HIGHLY EFFECTIVE SOCIAL IMPACT COMMUNICATORS ...
         ARE ASTUTE TRANSLATORS INSIDE AND OUTSIDE OF THEIR ORGANIZATIONS

Get comfortable standing out as a translator

The first thing I must do is to burst your bubble a bit. I suppose you can't really burst a bubble without going full tilt, so here goes: no one knows whether you're a square peg or a round hole.

Yes, you might have the title of CEO or chief marketing officer or communications manager. But if you are serious about practicing social impact communication as a craft, your title will not spare you.

You will stand out.

This is because you

- Tell stories in ways that highlight aspects of your organization's social impact leadership, rather than just its specific products, services, or projects

- Ask deeper questions to best understand how your organization's mission and desired outcomes align

- Engage internal and external stakeholders to align on the key talking points and words that will best make the message resonate at head and heart levels

- Imagine creative new ways to use data and storytelling to illustrate the journey your organization is on and the progress you're making

- Feel a sense of loyalty to all parties to get the social impact story right—and engage people to the point they're ready to take action

So what can you do when you don't feel as though you fit in?

First, recognize your role for what it is: a unique position of power. I'm not talking about stepping on other people or thinking of your role as more important than the roles of others. I'm simply suggesting that you

CHAPTER 2 SECRET #2: HIGHLY EFFECTIVE SOCIAL IMPACT COMMUNICATORS ...
ARE ASTUTE TRANSLATORS INSIDE AND OUTSIDE OF THEIR ORGANIZATIONS

have something of value and of the moment. The kinds of issues you're wrestling with are issues on the minds of people in your local community and around the world. For example, 76 percent of US registered voters seek bipartisan climate-change action, according to a Morning Consult poll commissioned by The Walton Family Foundation.[1]

This power means those around you are ready to listen to what you have to say. You have a responsibility to understand the nuances of the topics about which you communicate. If you are tasked with climate-change communication, you'll probably need to learn about the key issues in this discipline in your industry. You'll want to understand what your organization is doing to address climate change, how that looks in practice, and when on the calendar you've set milestones to achieve.

Once you have this kind of understanding, you can help bring perspective to the table. What are the best words, phrases, and concepts to share in your internal and external communications? Which words and concepts won't strike a chord—or might backfire in unexpected ways? Why do people care about this issue, and why now? What is your organization's unique perspective or set of experiences that gives it the voice people need to hear right now?

You now have power, perspective—and also strategy. Think of all the decisions you make in a day. To be an effective translational communicator, you must think several steps ahead. You must have relationships with the stakeholders, internally and externally, with whom you communicate. You must know the words they use, what stories they're telling, and how to help them see eye to eye with the stories of others.

When you can master this process, you will be ready for any ballet or samba placed on your figurative dance card at the office. Focus on

---

[1] "As America Marks 50th Anniversary of Clean Water Act, Poll Highlights Agriculture's Strong Connection to Water." October 18, 2022. The Walton Family Foundation. www.waltonfamilyfoundation.org/voters-want-sustainable-ag-practices-that-support-clean-water

CHAPTER 2   SECRET #2: HIGHLY EFFECTIVE SOCIAL IMPACT COMMUNICATORS ...
              ARE ASTUTE TRANSLATORS INSIDE AND OUTSIDE OF THEIR ORGANIZATIONS

managing your energy to move gracefully from one dance into another. You might be preparing a CEO briefing in the morning and developing collateral for external audiences in the afternoon. This is where serving as a translator, walking between worlds, can be an awful lot of fun.

The opportunity to serve as a translational communicator—to get clear on the views of multiple stakeholders and bring them more closely together—might sound thrilling. It also might sound like "Texas Chainsaw Massacre" meets "The Joy of Painting" with Bob Ross, a TV legend here in the states known for his iconic calm voice and gentle artwork. You might feel as though your world is being upended. You might feel a fearful sense of disruption that's about to throw your work life off the rails.

Yet I assure you, a social impact communicator who acts as a translator will have the upper hand in any conversation. Again, the point is not to attain some bizarre political advantage over another person. The point is to help you apply the empathy you naturally bring to social impact work to care for others and maintain momentum.

When you get clear on what others are saying and what they're meaning behind those words, you can become a helpful sherpa guiding both parties down the same path. Even if no one is holding hands, at least they're more unified in purpose and resolve.

Let's unpack why (and how) to do this most effectively. This enables you to put the chainsaws out of your mind and pick up the paintbrushes.

Why social impact communicators must learn to translate among parties—and how

There are several benefits of serving as a translator on a social impact team. Remember, social impact communication is not only a skill to cultivate but also a leadership discipline to practice. You are uniquely

CHAPTER 2   SECRET #2: HIGHLY EFFECTIVE SOCIAL IMPACT COMMUNICATORS ...
ARE ASTUTE TRANSLATORS INSIDE AND OUTSIDE OF THEIR ORGANIZATIONS

suited to use language to help people see eye to eye more clearly. The ellipses at the end are designed to lead into the following subheaders/H2s (e.g. ... Understand and recognize the worldviews, etc.)

... Understand and recognize the worldviews and unique sectoral cultures of different stakeholder types

As someone who has built and led multistakeholder social impact programs, I know firsthand what you too have probably discovered: different stakeholders see the world in different ways. Knowing how to read the room, understand the unique considerations informing each person's decisions, and appreciate the value their sector brings to the partnership is extremely important.

Three common entities engaged in social impact communication efforts are private-sector businesses, nonprofits, and government agencies. These groups frequently collaborate in the food and agriculture programs in which I have participated. To understand why your ability to translate is so important, let's consider their unique perspectives, their unique value, and the shared value with other collaborators that they each bring to partnerships. This example draws on my experience doing US-based social impact work.

Private-sector businesses

- **Unique perspective:** We bring novel products and services to market. Our reward is doing good while also making a profit.

- **Unique value:** We bring a commitment to creativity and proprietary innovation. We aim to meet the needs of our customers and our shareholders.

Nonprofits

- **Unique perspective:** We do mission-driven work in targeted focus areas for the good of our constituents and society. Our reward is doing good while also satisfying the mission and vision of the funders who empower our work.

- **Unique value:** We bring a commitment to education, research, programming, and advocacy for the public good. We aim to meet the needs of our program beneficiaries and our funding partners.

Government agencies

- **Unique perspective:** We implement the priorities of the acting presidential administration and its appointees, within the budgetary guidelines Congress approves. Our reward is doing good by properly stewarding and implementing the American taxpayer's dollars.

- **Unique value:** We aim to invest holistically across all Congressional districts, reaching and supporting as many diverse Americans as possible. We aim to meet the needs of the public and the agency's mission and leadership.

The preceding illustration is very basic and undoubtedly misses many nuances. But I am hopeful it conveys the point: Each type of stakeholder group is needed, and each views the world through different lenses *by the very nature of the organization's structure, history, and stated mission*. When you act as a translator, you take the initiative to learn and

CHAPTER 2   SECRET #2: HIGHLY EFFECTIVE SOCIAL IMPACT COMMUNICATORS ...
                ARE ASTUTE TRANSLATORS INSIDE AND OUTSIDE OF THEIR ORGANIZATIONS

appreciate these differences so you can effectively help leaders from each organization type find common ground and solve problems with the respective strengths of each party.

All of these groups share much in common, as well. For example, I bet you find that all of these stakeholder types:

- Value measurable and positive social impact outcomes
- Appreciate the role of data and technology to inform decisions and monitor progress
- Seek constructive feedback and open communication to forge stronger relationships and more effective programs of work

You can increase your effectiveness as a translator by learning about all of the stakeholder groups with whom you come into contact. Offer to meet 1:1 with key points of contact. Seek permission to ask questions and learn more about what they do—and why. Understand the parameters, rules, and regulations that determine what they can and can't do in a partnership. Learn where flexibility exists to get creative.

I promise, you won't regret investing your time this way.

... See both sides of an issue

Spoiler alert: Few issues in social impact communication are clear-cut. If I had to measure it out precisely in a recipe, I would say something like, "Pour approximately no cups of clarity into your batter. It will make things laughable, and no one will believe you."

If we all had the answers to the world's most pressing challenges, you would not be sitting here reading this book. You would have solved the problem and booked your tickets to someplace tropical. There, you would sit on a beach and imagine that the clouds look like dragons, or castles, or a map to a buried pot of gold beneath the rainbow.

CHAPTER 2   SECRET #2: HIGHLY EFFECTIVE SOCIAL IMPACT COMMUNICATORS ...
              ARE ASTUTE TRANSLATORS INSIDE AND OUTSIDE OF THEIR ORGANIZATIONS

But of course you don't have time to imagine beaches and leprechaun rainbows. You are actually busy parsing through the complexity of climate change or achieving greater racial equity or another societal issue of tremendous consequence.

With any big issue, there will be at least two sides, and frequently more. Social impact issues are not squares or rectangles. Rather, they are polyhedrons with the infinity symbol scrawled on them.

In the world of food and agriculture, climate has traditionally been a polarizing topic. "Polarizing" is perhaps the wrong word. Let's just say it has been the entrée to the subject of how food and agriculture can address a changing climate.

Some argue that voluntary carbon markets are the way to go. Farmers can sign up to implement new practices on acres they choose. These practices can lock carbon in the soil (though how much, or how for long, is the subject of ongoing study and debate). Farmers can sell those credits to corporate partners, who can count those environmental benefits toward their greenhouse gas emissions reduction targets. The farmer might get help such as an incentive payment or technical support or a gold star on a website. (I jest, but only just.)

There is at least one other school of thought. They view carbon markets as simply passing the buck. They say such markets encourage people who release emissions to take credit for someone else's savings while continuing to pollute.

Still others say carbon is a false flag. Really, they argue, there are far more important issues to deal with such as the degradation of wildlife habitat, the rapid depletion of groundwater, or, you know, pick a subject.

See what I mean by complexity?

Now consider your own industry. What are the key social impact practices, topics, or projects that keep people up at night where you work? Which activities and topics get them excited? From which topics would they run screaming if they were trapped in a room together? What do professionals in your industry see as the hero activities that could address

CHAPTER 2   SECRET #2: HIGHLY EFFECTIVE SOCIAL IMPACT COMMUNICATORS ... ARE ASTUTE TRANSLATORS INSIDE AND OUTSIDE OF THEIR ORGANIZATIONS

this social impact issue? Which activities do people in your industry love to vilify?

I'm not asking you to pick sides, nor am I asking you to be Switzerland to everyone else's United States. I'm simply offering the observation that as a social impact communicator, you are uniquely suited to be a translator. You are well versed in the different sides of an issue.

You have not only read books, magazine articles, professional newsletters, watched videos, and so on. You also have bothered to consider the unspoken truths or beliefs behind what's stated on videos, or marketing collateral, or social media. And you have an informed idea of how those messages are going to fall on different audiences. Some people celebrate the message and share it eagerly. Others laugh and publicly poke fun at it. Perhaps a legislator will weigh the message and propose a bill that, if adopted, changes the course of human history.

I'm being a bit dramatic. As a social impact communicator, you are investing time in ways others in your organization likely are not. For the most part, the executive leaders in your organization don't have time to consider the sea of messages happening in your chosen social impact space. The sales and marketing teams might pay a little attention, but their goals are likely different than yours. They might want to find messages of differentiation, but they might not be thinking about connecting with the heart and the head of their customers' values like you are.

You have the unique opportunity to step back, see the big picture, and understand the many possible messages competing in the marketplace of social impact ideas. Then, you get to decide which elements you would like to use, which you'd prefer to reject, and which messages need to be said and aren't making the cut. You get to apply creativity and decision-making. Your organization depends on you for this because no one else will do it. Some won't care to do it, and others simply don't have the time.

Whether you are crafting PR strategy, or developing an annual sustainability report, or completing a progress narrative for a philanthropist or government agency, see both (all) sides of an issue. Then weigh which angles and narratives will help you be truthful, accurate, and compelling as you present how your organization is addressing social impact issues.

Polarizing narratives have no place in the world of a social impact communicator. (Although be prepared: You are bound to always offend somebody.)

What has a place is people, and reality, and the promise of the opportunities toward which you are dancing. (See? Another dance analogy!) Tell that story, and you will do well.

… Explain a complex issue in ways many can understand

My wife, Dr. Julie Birt, is a scientist—or, as she jokingly refers to herself, a book doctor. Her specialty is science education. She helps college educators strategically deploy writing in the classroom to help students by reinforcing learning, opening their minds to new ideas, and achieving the intended outcomes of the class.

As Julie worked toward the completion of her PhD, I had the opportunity to read many academic papers. I even began to grasp the meaning of some of the content, if only faintly.

As social impact communicators, you and I often write in a slightly less technical way. Hurray for us, and hurray for the academy! We can both serve our respective audiences in our respective lanes.

Yet there is something to be said for academic writing. If you happen to be an educator who also is a social impact communicator, I applaud you. I admire scientific writing for its clarity, its point-by-point analysis of an issue, its detailed methodology, and the forward-looking findings and proposed future research recommendations. This beautiful narrative arc graces the pages of academic journals the world over. It's a shared language and process for making meaning out of complexity.

CHAPTER 2 SECRET #2: HIGHLY EFFECTIVE SOCIAL IMPACT COMMUNICATORS ...
ARE ASTUTE TRANSLATORS INSIDE AND OUTSIDE OF THEIR ORGANIZATIONS

Social impact communicators must make meaning out of complexity for the sake of both written and spoken communication. Remember, your role is both as a communicator and as a leader.

For example, if your field of work is focused on addressing climate change, you probably have studied the various types of emissions that can contribute to a warming world. You probably understand the key contributors of emissions in your industry. You might have initially researched this for a white paper or a social media campaign or similar. Or you might have studied it deeply to field questions from investors at a quarterly call.

Yet your use of complex knowledge doesn't end here. Instead, it must often carry over into other decisions you are asked to make. For example, you might have to work with colleagues and partners to wrestle with questions such as the following:

- What position will our organization take on this complex or even controversial issue?

- Who needs to be at the table to make this decision?

- What are the second- and third-order implications of this decision—if we are right and if we are wrong?

- How often should we revisit this particular issue for potentially new developments, research studies, or commonly held opinions in our industry?

By using your translational communication skills to navigate complexity, you have the potential to influence many stakeholders in your organization. These include the following:

- C-suite leaders who often must make public and long-lasting decisions about how your organization will invest its financial and personnel resources in social impact

- Midlevel managers leading teams who are doing the work of social impact implementation

- Communication professionals whose social impact content including marketing and communications collateral will build off your foundation

- New employees who want to know what you stand for in social impact

- Veteran employees skeptical of new things, such as social impact

- External partners watching you closely on your stance and actions around social impact

Translators take into account not only the complexity of the social impact issue but also the complexity of the audiences they serve. They consider the role they will play in deciding how the work of social impact gets done.

Use your influence wisely. Choose your words with care rooted in careful study and reflection. Recognize that you can always adapt your path as new information emerges.

... Define your personal views on the social impact issues you help solve

Effective social impact communicators recognize that their mindset is malleable and ever changing. Translating within and outside of your organization grows your adaptability. It helps you critically think about the social impact issues your organization addresses.

In my professional life, I have had plenty of opportunities for this kind of soul searching. I've spent most of my time around leaders in business, nonprofits, and the government who are united in their commitment to

CHAPTER 2   SECRET #2: HIGHLY EFFECTIVE SOCIAL IMPACT COMMUNICATORS ...
ARE ASTUTE TRANSLATORS INSIDE AND OUTSIDE OF THEIR ORGANIZATIONS

fighting climate change. Yet I've also met other leaders, particularly out in farm country, who are guarded or even skeptical about the degree to which humans can prevent climate change.

In some cases, your organization will take a position on an issue. In other cases, it might prefer to not take a position—at least externally.

Your role as a social impact communicator is to be well studied on the topic. Your obligation is to speak up and advocate for what you know to be right and true based on your unique insights. You should use your best professional communicator voice. Then, you must honor the organization's decision—or, if you must, choose to go elsewhere if you and your organization are in conflict.

This isn't a book on finding a new job, so I won't dwell on this point. But I hope the spirit of the message resonates with you. Social impact communicators are not activists in a sign-carrying sense, nor are they rugs that fall flat under the compulsion of others.

Rather, they (you!) are engaged professionals. You are well versed in the social impact issues of the day. You advocate for the right thing. You recognize that you can influence the social impact decisions of your organization, up to a point.

As I see it, the doctor's oath of "First, do no harm" applies beautifully here. If you are a social impact communicator who has some decision-making capacity, but not all of it, put this into practice. (And P.S. Almost every social impact communicator, whether you are a CEO or midlevel director or a communications manager, is in some way dependent on other parties to reach a decision.)

Think through things widely and deeply in your own mind. Care enough to have conviction of your own ideas, and speak up and share them as appropriate, as you build more trust and influence.

At the same time, recognize you are part of an organization and potentially many projects or partnerships. You have a responsibility to serve the greater good. Even though you won't always agree with every decision, remember

CHAPTER 2   SECRET #2: HIGHLY EFFECTIVE SOCIAL IMPACT COMMUNICATORS ...
         ARE ASTUTE TRANSLATORS INSIDE AND OUTSIDE OF THEIR ORGANIZATIONS

- First, do no harm.
- Then, resolve to engage, heart and mind, with the humans you work alongside to do more good, more often, time and again.

... Build the most compelling case in partnership with others

I can build a defensible multimillion-dollar social impact program budget. I can defend it with compelling evidence so that the work can commence. But it wasn't always that way.

During my career, mentors have taught me how to ensure Is are dotted and Ts crossed in social impact program budgets. (Even in the mission-driven, purpose-focused field of social impact, having money in the bank is often the difference between doing good and doing nothing at all. And I wanted to do a fair bit more than nothing.)

At first, I tried building budgets and met with modest success. Then, I'd spot a problem and pour forth apologies for errors I'd inserted into a spreadsheet. This approach might make you feel as if you've taken your lumps, but it does little translational good.

I made the fastest progress when I studied the budget, came up with questions I couldn't answer, and asked leaders and peers on my team for help. They helped me pull a social impact budget apart and put it back together again so we could achieve our goals. I could then get back to the communications strategy and content development work I loved.

As a social impact communicator, doing your homework comes naturally. You have studied the complexities of your social impact effort and formed your own opinions. You are able to help others move the organization's mission forward.

One day, the task will fall to you to explain your organization's social impact mission first to your colleagues, and then to your leaders,

CHAPTER 2   SECRET #2: HIGHLY EFFECTIVE SOCIAL IMPACT COMMUNICATORS ...
              ARE ASTUTE TRANSLATORS INSIDE AND OUTSIDE OF THEIR ORGANIZATIONS

and then to the external partners, clients, and other organizations that depend on you.

You're not a Midwestern-nice-excuse-maker. You're a change-maker.

When you can translate what you are doing into a language others can understand, you have passed the first test. When you have mastered the "so that" and can articulate it, you have passed the final exam.

... Stay humble and stay focused on the mission

In life and at work, I have often found myself in the uncomfortable position of telephone operator. By this, I mean that Person A (let's call him Fred) and Person B (let's call her Barb) aren't getting along. Or at least they don't see the same issue the same way.

Fred approaches me first.

"Please tell Barb that her way just isn't going to fly, and she needs to do things differently," he says. (You might have a Fred or a Barb in your life. Insert those names into this example.)

"My, that sounds sort of harsh," I reply. "Are you sure you don't want to say it this way [insert a series of words, translated into a framework that works for Fred] instead?"

"Wow, I never considered that," Fred replies. "That's right. I'll say it that way."

Fred and Barb talk, and they work things out beautifully, and they go and get ice cream afterward.

If only workplace scenarios like these unfolded this way. It would be a dream!

The reality, though, is that many times things don't go so smoothly, with minimal confrontation. There might be bumps—and confrontation.

This is a humbling experience. As a social impact communicator, you might have to relay an especially uncomfortable message. You might even agree with the message but prefer that somebody else deliver it.

CHAPTER 2   SECRET #2: HIGHLY EFFECTIVE SOCIAL IMPACT COMMUNICATORS ...
ARE ASTUTE TRANSLATORS INSIDE AND OUTSIDE OF THEIR ORGANIZATIONS

There will come a day, though, when that somebody will be you. What will you do? You will embrace your role as a translator, which includes an attitude of humility. And you will deliver the unpleasant message as best you know how so the mission can advance.

Perhaps you are sharing difficult news that someone's job is in jeopardy if they don't change their actions. Or maybe you have just learned that a much-sought-after funding round is going toward someone else's project, not yours. There are a thousand possibilities.

When we are translating a tough message for others, it's tempting to focus on the strong emotions the message evokes. Perhaps it's fear or anger or confusion. That's only natural.

What I want you, the astute social impact communicator, to do is to reframe your mindset to focus on how the message will help the mission proceed.

Yes, of course you should think carefully about the words to use and about the person who will be hearing them. You should consider how the other person might respond.

Then, you must stick your chin a bit higher in the sky and resolve to move ahead with the conversation anyway. It is the right thing to do.

Attention to the mission focuses you on others and on getting the work right the first time. In lieu of that, a thoughtful translator learns from mistakes and improves their performance the second and third time. Translation, even when it's hardest to execute, keeps you focused and serious. It compels you forward. It reminds you why you are doing this work. It reinforces why you are doing this work with this specific team that you serve alongside.

CHAPTER 2   SECRET #2: HIGHLY EFFECTIVE SOCIAL IMPACT COMMUNICATORS ...
ARE ASTUTE TRANSLATORS INSIDE AND OUTSIDE OF THEIR ORGANIZATIONS

... Mold exactly the right team for the work you're doing

I'll have much more to say about the importance of teamwork in the work of any effective social impact communicator later in this book. For now, understand that when you become a master of translation, you are effectively mastering the leadership needed to mold a team that does excellent social impact work.

You gain this skill, whether on purpose or by regular practice, because you are applying the fundamentals of leadership. You make a conscious choice to

- Listen to your teammates
- Understand their needs and talents
- Ask questions
- Delegate opportunities
- Follow through
- Learn from wins and losses
- Motivate your team and partners and recognize their essential contributions to the mission's success

When you walk between worlds, you understand where every team member fits and how they are making your organization's social impact work possible. You appreciate the positive energy they bring—what author Jon Gordon describes as "the optimism, trust, enthusiasm, love, purpose, joy, passion, and spirit to live, work, and perform at a higher level."[2]

---

[2] Gordon, Jon. "The Energy Bus: 10 Rules to Fuel Your Life, Work, and Team with Positive Energy." May 18, 2009. www.amazon.com/Energy-Bus-Rules-Fuel-Positive-ebook/dp/B0086I25S8/ref=sr_1_1?crid=1X7JKN4YXELUL&keywords=energy+bus+book+by+jon+gordon&qid=1682528331&sprefix=energy+bus%2Caps%2C119&sr=8-1&asin=B0086I25S8&revisionId=8b93ad96&format=1&depth=1

CHAPTER 2   SECRET #2: HIGHLY EFFECTIVE SOCIAL IMPACT COMMUNICATORS ...
ARE ASTUTE TRANSLATORS INSIDE AND OUTSIDE OF THEIR ORGANIZATIONS

The age of barking orders is rapidly collapsing, at least I am hopeful this is the case. The new era of social impact teams requires skilled communicators who listen to things happening in the world. They apply those insights to their organization's unique social impact mission. Then, they bring into community the people inside their organization for just the right role.

Teamwork frequently crosses beyond the boundaries of your real or virtual office, too. More and more, social impact projects bring together multiple organizations—often with little in common and almost zero history of working together—to carry out the work.

In my career, I've been privileged to build several social impact coalitions. I didn't know the first thing about bringing people together around a common goal. But I did know how to appreciate the unique talents of each organization and its team. I could engage in conversation with people I'd spent little time with. As a curious person, I knew how to ask questions. I could pull what I'd learned onto a printed page and formulate a meaningful proposal that illustrated ways we could work together.

Sure enough, we quickly had the makings of a program that enabled business owners in our industry to go further faster. Translation kept our conversations flowing and aligned our unique interests toward a common goal.

You have what it takes to mold teams to do great work, too. You are a translational communicator, someone who gets things done while walking between worlds.

All it takes is some firm anchoring with the hearts and minds of the people who are best equipped for the work ahead.

CHAPTER 2   SECRET #2: HIGHLY EFFECTIVE SOCIAL IMPACT COMMUNICATORS ...
ARE ASTUTE TRANSLATORS INSIDE AND OUTSIDE OF THEIR ORGANIZATIONS

... Achieve diverse social impact outcomes across different industries amid rapid change

I used to worry that my decade-long focus on food and agriculture might be a liability. What if I wanted to become a construction expert, or a forestry leader, or a circus performer? How would I possibly pick up and take with me everything I had learned? What exactly would be relevant or uniquely qualifying about my deep subject matter expertise?

It turns out that much of what I learned is highly transferable to other industries. I suspect this is true for you, too.

Social impact communication is a new discipline, but that doesn't make it an obscure discipline. The ability to translate across teams and engage, human to human, with hearts and heads will serve you wherever you go. This is true whether you make a career at your current organization or pursue social impact goals somewhere else.

Everyone I've met in this space wants to do good. They want an outlet for their passion and commitment to the cause. They relish working with others who are similarly dedicated. They love trading ideas, learning new things, boiling their knowledge into actionable insights, and being challenged by new perspectives.

Does this describe you? When you cultivate the discipline of translation, no matter where you sit in your organization, you are building a toolbox that will serve you wherever you choose to set up shop.

Now more than ever, your contributions matter. You are helping organizations get better at talking to themselves. You are helping the rest of us understand what your organization does and why it matters. You are painting portraits that help us see what the world of tomorrow will look like.

And why we should all get excited to be part of it.

CHAPTER 2 SECRET #2: HIGHLY EFFECTIVE SOCIAL IMPACT COMMUNICATORS ...
ARE ASTUTE TRANSLATORS INSIDE AND OUTSIDE OF THEIR ORGANIZATIONS

... Find a home within your organization and among your peers at last

Back in 2016, I had the privilege of visiting China on a tour of farms and agriculture in the country. I found it incredible to see how Chinese farmers operated on relatively small parcels of land compared to American producers. I sat in as leaders spoke about how the farmers in their community worked together, how they shared equipment, why they were interested in expanding their investments in dairy.

But I also remember another feeling that accompanied the fascination: isolation. It dawned on me shortly after arriving at the Beijing airport that I was, quite literally, on the opposite side of the world from my home in Missouri. The weight of the separation I felt had never struck me with such force. If I needed to get to my family right away, I simply couldn't. The physical distance and the Pacific Ocean sat between us.

Being a social impact communicator within your organization can feel a bit gut-wrenching. You can experience a sense of aloneness and of being far apart from others. Some people might not get your mission. They might think you're commanding an awful lot of resources for little or no financial return. They might feel they're being shorted in favor of your (perceived) excess.

Yet when you embrace your role as a translator, something fascinating happens. It's even more fascinating than the fact that many people around the world drink their tea with loose leaves that fall to the bottom of their drinking glasses. (I suddenly feel a hint of disdain for my Americanized tea bags and fruity flavorings.)

The fascinating thing is this: As a social impact translator, you cultivate relationships and find areas of commonality with other people. You start to know your colleagues as human beings first—people who have families, friends, hobbies, and dreams. In many cases, your peers will start to see the same qualities in you.

CHAPTER 2   SECRET #2: HIGHLY EFFECTIVE SOCIAL IMPACT COMMUNICATORS ...
            ARE ASTUTE TRANSLATORS INSIDE AND OUTSIDE OF THEIR ORGANIZATIONS

Translation is not a transactional activity designed to help your social impact team steamroll other divisions and departments at a faster rate. It is a tool that brings us into community. It surrounds us with a shared language. It empowers us to care about the mission (see Chapter 1) and especially about one another.

When we care about one another, we can do truly magical work.

How translation has served my social impact journey so far

As I have worked with clients in various industries, I have found that translation quickly builds bridges to doing important work. In meetings underpinned with skilled translators, participants

- Appreciate the respective strengths of the people in the physical and virtual rooms where they meet
- Get more deliberate in their conversations
- Acknowledge the realities and complexities of running complex social impact programs
- Prioritize the scheduling of future check-ins
- Share progress reports and learnings to ensure maximum effectiveness
- Solicit input from key stakeholders to ensure social impact efforts meet their needs, first and foremost
- Imagine what else they might do together in the future

Whatever your social impact mission, recognize and appreciate the leadership and communication roles you play as a social impact communicator. Step back from the canvas you are painting to stand in awe of what you have created using the skill of translation—and of what the final masterpiece will look like.

CHAPTER 2   SECRET #2: HIGHLY EFFECTIVE SOCIAL IMPACT COMMUNICATORS ...
             ARE ASTUTE TRANSLATORS INSIDE AND OUTSIDE OF THEIR ORGANIZATIONS

Highly effective social impact communicators become translators on purpose. Because translators build connections and connections foster relationships.

And when we prioritize the right relationships, we can do anything we set our minds to do.

That's because our values are crystal clear and point us due north. And it's to those ever-important values that we turn our attention next.

Key Questions

- What are your greatest communication skills? Which skills are you most focused on growing?

- Where is the need for translational communication greatest within your organization? Outside of it? What have you found most effective at bridging understanding gaps?

- What small habits might you implement to grow your ability to "walk between worlds" in your social impact work?

- What first step might you take to better understand the various stakeholder types with whom you do social impact work? What questions will you ask to better understand how they make decisions—and how you can most effectively work together?

- What's one thing you might do in the next 30 days to help a peer, a leader, or another team member grow their own translation capabilities? How might this benefit you, your organization, your partners, and the mission?

CHAPTER 3

Secret #3: Highly effective social impact communicators … leverage the strength of personal and organizational values to tell compelling stories

For communicators I know and love, neglect is among the greatest on-the-job hazards. Let me tell you why this is dangerous.

Well, first, let me explain what I mean by neglect. I am not referring to the way social impact communicators treat their families or their work

CHAPTER 3   SECRET #2: HIGHLY EFFECTIVE SOCIAL IMPACT COMMUNICATORS ...
ARE ASTUTE TRANSLATORS INSIDE AND OUTSIDE OF THEIR ORGANIZATIONS

colleagues. On the contrary, professionals who focus on social impact issues at work tend to be standup people, in my experience.

After all: If they didn't care about their families and their colleagues, how could they possibly talk about healing the environment, or achieving greater equity? Maybe they could, but it would be inauthentic.

No, the neglect I'm referencing is much more personal. You pour everything you have into the technical side of your job. Then, you neglect your heart and soul.

I get it because I've done it. We communicators want to ensure we cultivate a vibrant and robust storehouse of ideas, story angles, sources, and perspectives.

We feed this need through research, interviews, and the very writing we commit to papers, to emails, to reports, and to ourselves in those never-ending to-do lists.

Meanwhile, we put our feelings on hold. We put our emotions out to pasture. We ignore our intuition. We disregard the weight of our experiences. Instead, we focus on churning out strategy, content, and social impact programs. We operate with the precision of a manufacturing plant.

I have nothing against manufacturing. Many of my favorite things began on an assembly line: my printed books, my car, my vintage pop-up camper, my children. (Well, I haven't quite figured out where children come from. They each seem to be programmed differently. And they never come with instruction manuals.)

In our rush to save the world or to help our employers and partners and customers feel the weight of what we are doing, we forget to pause. We don't reflect on what uniquely qualifies us for the work.

In this chapter, I'm going to get you feeling comfortable, confident, and enthusiastic about bringing your best self to the work of social impact communications. Who you are and what you do derives in large part from the values you hold. These are the pillars of your personal beliefs that guide your words, your actions, and the lenses through which you see the world.

CHAPTER 3   SECRET #2: HIGHLY EFFECTIVE SOCIAL IMPACT COMMUNICATORS ...
                ARE ASTUTE TRANSLATORS INSIDE AND OUTSIDE OF THEIR ORGANIZATIONS

Let's begin by moving away from the assembly-line mentality and toward a cozier place filled with rich potential: your own personal workshop.

The place where values come from is the workshop inside your head—and inside your organization

I didn't want to build the chicken run or the 630-ft. fence in my backyard. Every time I considered these projects, I got heart palpitations. I started to sweat. My anxiety went through the roof.

My wife, Julie, reassured me these projects needed to be done to help the homestead. She blueprinted everything. She gave me the list of supplies we'd need, which I ordered from the local lumber company. I journeyed to the farm store and hoisted, with the help of a nice associate, a 7,000-lb. (or so it seemed) roll of cattle panel wire into the back of our beloved silver Subaru.

My mind and muscles ached. I hadn't even set the first post in the ground.

The chickens needed a run so they could peck for grain and live their best life because raccoons had decimated the flock weeks before. To make matters worse, we had been on vacation 800 miles from the scene of the crime.

We vowed this sort of thing would never happen again. We would fortify the chickens inside of Fort Knox-A-Bawk. The fence project came later and enabled us to let our two big pups, a Great Pyrenees mix and a hunting dog, run free without running freely into the neighbors' yards.

Intellectually, I understood the importance of the work. Julie had done her homework. The animals clearly needed our help. But I had some fundamental misunderstanding about my values. This spawned what author and creativity champion Steven Pressfield calls resistance.

CHAPTER 3   SECRET #2: HIGHLY EFFECTIVE SOCIAL IMPACT COMMUNICATORS ...
ARE ASTUTE TRANSLATORS INSIDE AND OUTSIDE OF THEIR ORGANIZATIONS

You might also encounter resistance as you dig deep into your values and the values of the company, nonprofit, or agency in which you work as a social impact communicator. Because we so seldom stop to consider what's driving us and our organizations, we often don't know the full breadth and depth of what we hold to be true. We fail to appreciate what our organization's founders, leaders, and other stakeholders value most.

You can participate in a simple thought exercise to come to grips with your own values and to better appreciate the values of your organization. By spending time with them, you will begin to appreciate yourself and your organization in a new way. Turn these values over in your hands. Examine their soft handles and their sharp edges. Take a look at any values that served you once and now are gathering dust. Consider which of your organization's values you implement daily and which might be deserving of closer attention and action.

The more deeply you appreciate this ecosystem of values, the more you can bring each into the light, out of the shadows. In turn, you bring a new depth of commitment, compassion, and creativity to the social impact communication you lead. What's more, you become a more influential and confident ambassador of your organization's deeply held values.

Welcome to the workshop of your mind.

The first thing to recognize about your workshop is that it probably isn't the cleanest place you've ever been. There are tales in the dust, though. Everything you find in this cobwebby, generous space has a purpose. It delivers value if you let it.

On the tool bench that sits against the wall of your workshop are the tools you and your organization use all the time. These represent the values you esteem most.

My parents, Norman and Anita, instilled in me some of the deepest values I hold today. They gave me the confidence to use them with pride and precision. These included the following:

CHAPTER 3   SECRET #2: HIGHLY EFFECTIVE SOCIAL IMPACT COMMUNICATORS ...
ARE ASTUTE TRANSLATORS INSIDE AND OUTSIDE OF THEIR ORGANIZATIONS

- **Work ethic:** Birts roll up their sleeves and get to the task with vigor. They ask, "What can I help with next?"

- **Faithful:** Birts are people of faith who honor God and honor all people as His creation.

- **Kindness:** Birts treat others with love, hospitality, care, and concern.

- **Humor:** Birts recognize life is too short to take things too seriously.

- **Honor:** Birts value and respect parents, grandparents, unrelated seniors, and people of diverse backgrounds and belief systems.

What values shaped your upbringing? Consider the kinds of things you heard your parents, or a trusted person in your life, say over the years. What did you observe about people you admired and respected? How did they treat others? How did they treat themselves? What made them stand out in a crowd?

The values we form over time and continue to nurture eventually mature and gain nuance. Just as the stones in a flowing stream displace water and cause it to rise up and down, so too do our values mold and shape how we appear to the outside world.

Now consider the values of your organization. If your organization doesn't have stated values (unlikely but possible), I bet you can observe them at work. For example, my social impact clients reflect values such as the following:

- **Innovation:** They solve problems in creative ways with the people, expertise, and tools their organization maintains and cultivates.

- **Integrity:** They develop products, services, and programs with honor and decency, designing them to genuinely help other organizations and individuals.

53

CHAPTER 3   SECRET #2: HIGHLY EFFECTIVE SOCIAL IMPACT COMMUNICATORS ...
            ARE ASTUTE TRANSLATORS INSIDE AND OUTSIDE OF THEIR ORGANIZATIONS

- **Vision:** They spend time thinking about what's coming next—and positioning themselves to meet those social impact needs.

- **Purpose:** They prize greater equity and a healthier environment above profit or other forms of financial performance without neglecting those details.

- **Leadership:** They recognize the special place they hold in their respective industry and use it to make lasting change with wide benefits.

There are also values less obvious to us. These are hidden in the shadows of our workshop.

You ought to examine these, too. They tend to be beliefs you treat as gospel because of a negative comment or a traumatic event. These values might actually turn out to be something useful, but not in their current condition. A saw caked in dust might turn out to be a hammer. Unless we examine these dubious values, we won't know for sure.

I can attest to this. For years, I held several less-than-optimal values until I started to examine them. I pulled them off their hanger on the wall and brushed off the dust. Occasionally, I gave these unpleasant values a good bath in soapy water or a touchup to remove rust. These included the following:

- **Bookish, not brawnish:** Exercise is more important for the mind than the body.

- **Utility lite:** Some people are good at fixing and building things. I am not one of them.

- **Career or calling:** You can feed your family or pursue the life of a starving artist, but not both.

- **Shared everything:** All people fundamentally see the world the same way.

- **Comfort equals happiness:** The best things in life happen when everything is calm and at rest.

Poke around in your mental workshop long enough and you find some of these dusty values—or others like them—stand quietly at attention hoping they will not be found out.

It's your job as a social impact communicator to do better than that. Pull those tools off the wall, or out of the drawer, or down from the shelf, and interrogate them.

It turns out exercise actually makes me feel good. It gives me greater confidence I'll have enough upper body strength to hold my grandchildren one day.

It turns out handiness is a skill you can pick up from others or learn on the fly. It's not coded into my genes.

It turns out you can bring your career and your calling closer together without missing a meal.

It turns out people have vastly different everything—upbringings, experiences, economic circumstances, political persuasions, and religious instruction.

It turns out the greatest growth and the biggest transformations I've experienced happened in times of upheaval and friction.

Hold onto your values while also brushing up those that don't serve you. Ask people you respect about the values they hold to be true. Invite them to answer a few questions, if they're comfortable doing so.

If your organization holds values—explicit or implicit—that you think might need work, get curious and explore why. Are those values really bad or simply different from your own? What experiences or market shifts might have contributed to those values? If a particular value needs work or refining, what might you do individually to start the conversation without criticizing something you don't fully understand?

CHAPTER 3 SECRET #2: HIGHLY EFFECTIVE SOCIAL IMPACT COMMUNICATORS ... ARE ASTUTE TRANSLATORS INSIDE AND OUTSIDE OF THEIR ORGANIZATIONS

Ask questions and be open to learning about the past, present, and developing values of your organization. Be principled while remaining open to the possibility that you can still function effectively in an organization whose values are not identical to your own.

This mindset enables you to build stronger relationships, personally and professionally. It also helps you consider whether you have some blind spots surrounding your values. Every workshop has an attic, and it often takes a friend or mentor to help you find the light switch. Together, you can dig through the clutter for new values that might serve your social impact mission. Ask your friend questions such as the following:

- What top three values define how you live your life? Why those values?

- What values did you once hold that turned out not to be true?

- Based on our relationship, how would you describe *my* values? Which serve me well? Which might need to be reimagined or removed?

The purpose of this exercise is not to make you or your friend uncomfortable. Instead, it's an exercise to keep you accountable for having an open mind.

The more awake you are to the person you call "me, myself, and I," the greater the potential of your social impact work. The more self-aware you become, the more you appreciate how your values and those of your organization can exist side by side—and even be mutually beneficial to one another.

You also experience a greater sense of peace that you have brought your whole self to the tasks at hand while honoring your organization's rich values.

CHAPTER 3   SECRET #2: HIGHLY EFFECTIVE SOCIAL IMPACT COMMUNICATORS ...
ARE ASTUTE TRANSLATORS INSIDE AND OUTSIDE OF THEIR ORGANIZATIONS

And if, in the worst-case scenario, you decide to leave your organization and pursue another that better aligns with your values system, that's OK, too.

Highly effective social impact communicators recognize that personal values and organizational ones can synchronize and strengthen one another.

My wish for you is just such an environment.

What power do values really have?

The thing about values is that they only have the power given to them by the master builder—that's you.

A drill is merely a museum artifact unless you remove it from its holster, plug in the battery, add a bit, and hold the tool just so. Squeezing the trigger causes the head of the drill to spin so the bit can eat away at the wood.

Values operate on a similar principle. You can say you believe in truth, justice, and the [insert your country here] way. But if you say one thing and do another, you are simply a hypocrite. Values grow as dull as an unused tool unless we pick them up and put them to work.

The power is in the people who bring them to life. The power is in you.

But how can we apply this to our social impact communications? What would the power of values look and feel like? My friend Dennis, a master craftsman and skilled user of tools, likes to say, "Measure twice, cut once."

The first thing you and I must do when it comes to putting our values to work as social impact communicators is to assess which values are appropriate to the mission. Then, we must make sure that all of the necessary values are present. And chances are good that others around us—on our teams, among our clients and partners, or in our customer base—will have complementary values to our own. (Not always. More on that in a moment.)

CHAPTER 3   SECRET #2: HIGHLY EFFECTIVE SOCIAL IMPACT COMMUNICATORS ... ARE ASTUTE TRANSLATORS INSIDE AND OUTSIDE OF THEIR ORGANIZATIONS

This process requires you to think critically. I'm not for a moment encouraging you to treat values like expendable masks you can put on and take off whenever the mood strikes you. I'm simply pointing out that some values give you greater energy, clarity, momentum, and creativity than others.

Let me give you an example. On several occasions, my clients who work in climate change communications have shared they want their children to inherit a better world. They want to do whatever they can to reverse a changing climate and avoid the risks scientists tell us are possible and predictable. These let's-please-avoids include greater heat, deeper cold, higher incidents of severe weather, shifts in crop production regions, and the need to put everyone on a shuttle bound for Mars.

If I were to go below the surface of this desire—to create a better world for our children—several values might emerge. I imagine those values include the following:

- **Compassion:** I care for others. I show people love and concern.

- **Conviction:** I try to pursue the right thing.

- **Stewardship:** It's up to me to take care of nature. My generation only gets one shot at this.

- **Nurture:** I brought my children into the world. It's up to me to take care of them.

- **Higher Calling:** I'm part of a bigger story. I must do my part to make things better for everyone.

An opposing set of values might lead us in a different direction. Imagine if you were a social impact communicator embittered by a lack of progress on climate change. (If this describes you, I promise—your secret is safe with me). You might embrace a different set of values from the one I described a moment ago. Your decidedly darker values could include the following:

CHAPTER 3   SECRET #2: HIGHLY EFFECTIVE SOCIAL IMPACT COMMUNICATORS ... ARE ASTUTE TRANSLATORS INSIDE AND OUTSIDE OF THEIR ORGANIZATIONS

- **Fear:** I'm running out of time. Whatever I do is too little, too late.

- **Hesitation:** I shouldn't just jump into something. I need to wait and see whether this approach is the right one.

- **Subsistence:** I'm going to stick it out right here, planted to this spot, to see if the world around me rises to the occasion.

- **Self-Preservation:** I'll do what it takes for my family, but I can't see the point in trying to make things better for everyone else.

- **Sorrow:** The losses I've already experienced outweigh any potential future gains.

Maybe you've worked with people who hold these types of values, both positive and problematic.

On the one hand, there are ebullient and optimistic people at all levels of an organization. They see the need to make a difference and recognize their role in doing so. They have awakened themselves to what they do best and how they can contribute to something big, bold, and important.

On the other hand, there are people—again, at all levels of an organization—who feel much differently. Their life experiences and personal reflections have led them down a darker path. Maybe they've lost sight of the values that brought them joy. Perhaps they've forgotten there are values within them that can make a positive difference for others and the wider world.

The most effective social impact communicators see the possibilities in both scenarios.

They recognize the workshop inside their minds contains vast stores of values and tools. Each tool can be used for good or for inertia—in other words, for standing still.

CHAPTER 3   SECRET #2: HIGHLY EFFECTIVE SOCIAL IMPACT COMMUNICATORS ...
            ARE ASTUTE TRANSLATORS INSIDE AND OUTSIDE OF THEIR ORGANIZATIONS

You can swing a hammer, or let it rest gently on the workbench gathering dust.

The best social impact communicators recognize the incredible energy values give them. They put a song in their heart and a vision in their head for what the future could look like. Whenever they have a bad day or feel discouraged by the latest headline, they return to their workshop. There, in earnest, seek a transformation. By doing this, they

- Turn **Fear** into **Compassion,** recognizing that love for others and the wider world drives out the things that haunt us

- Shift from **Hesitation** into **Conviction**, understanding strong values are an unstoppable force

- Move from **Subsistence** into **Stewardship**, seeing the promise of actively caring for those around them, in word and in action

- Abandon **Self-Preservation** and pursue **Nurture**, honoring others with their time and talents

- Forego **Sorrow** in favor of a **Higher Calling**, which allows them to leave what's hurting or missing and pursue all of the wonderful possibilities ahead

Values are the power tools of the highly effective social impact communicator. When you appreciate their transformative potential, you are ready to take the next step.

It's time to place those tools into a toolbox and leave the comfort of your workshop in search of the people, places, and projects that need your help.

CHAPTER 3   SECRET #2: HIGHLY EFFECTIVE SOCIAL IMPACT COMMUNICATORS ...
ARE ASTUTE TRANSLATORS INSIDE AND OUTSIDE OF THEIR ORGANIZATIONS

Define the solutions you offer as a social impact communicator

No one I know holds the title "social impact communicator." Which is funny, given the title of this book. The reality is that social impact communication is a skill set that pairs words and leadership, as I've noted already.

But imagine if you put out a shingle as a social impact communicator. How would you describe the kinds of solutions you provide? If you were to put your toolbox in your car and travel to the jobsite to get to work, what kinds of things would you do under the blazing sun? (Or, if you prefer, in the climate-controlled office with your cup of single-source coffee?)

You have your own answers. Here is my short list based on my experience consulting on social impact communication across many industries.

Writing

I personally gravitate to this one first. It's often the most comfortable solution a social impact communicator provides because it's familiar, like a pair of warm slippers inviting us home. Writing looks like crafting emails, building communications campaigns, preparing white papers, and writing research reports.

Editing

This solution involves modifying a communications message to fit its desired audience. (I started by writing "target audience" and then deleted it. Who wants to be on the business end of a weaponized term?) It could be a written message or video content or a story in any format, really. When you edit, you carefully consider the audience and how they think.

You modify the message in an effort to achieve an intended result. This could include building understanding on a topic, inviting someone to sign up for a program, or encouraging a friend to share a news item.

Facilitating

Many social impact communicators I know bring people together—within their division, across their organization, or across partner organizations. You provide a solution that requires a complex mix of disciplines and perspectives. You shepherd conversations with the goal of getting someplace new and better.

Leading

You might mentor colleagues, hire team members, or meet with prospective funders. All of these activities make up the solution of leading. Words, conversation, and relationship building are the building blocks that make great social impact leadership possible.

Empowering

You know your elevated profile and the nature of your social impact mission requires behavior at a higher standard. Not only do you perform a job with social impact benefits. You also inspire people and encourage them to keep going as you partner on advancing the mission. The manufacturing mentality I mentioned earlier has no place in the world of social impact. Social impact communicators actively seek to disassemble the Old Order of assembly-line impact in favor of the New Order. In the New Order, people treat other people like humans and leverage the renewable energy of teamwork to make it so. We'll discuss that in the next chapter, I promise.

CHAPTER 3   SECRET #2: HIGHLY EFFECTIVE SOCIAL IMPACT COMMUNICATORS ...
ARE ASTUTE TRANSLATORS INSIDE AND OUTSIDE OF THEIR ORGANIZATIONS

Building

Your imagination and creativity are central to your work as a social impact communicator. This is true whether you are designing a grant proposal or reimagining how a social impact program can deliver more predictable outcomes. Building looks like designing things from whole cloth or reworking existing systems so more people benefit from the work you do.

Want to be more effective? Pair the right value(s) to the right social impact solutions

You now know some of the common functions of social impact communicators. I bet none of them came as a surprise to you.

You're probably shouting at me from the comfort of your chair.

"I can think of ten more things I do beyond this list!" you scream. "Do you think I sit around all day and eat bonbons?"

Decidedly, no. I am confident I have barely held a candle to the important work you do. The point is these are some big umbrella solutions you undoubtedly deliver each day. So do I in my consulting business.

It would be easy to stop there. You've identified the values you hold precious. You've assessed the kinds of solutions you provide. Now, go and do it!

But it's not that simple. If it were, you would enjoy the company of happier colleagues, find deeper satisfaction at work, and have more to show for all that investment of time and energy.

Instead what you have (if I were to guess) is an imperfect workplace in which some people don't particularly care whether your values and your solutions fit hand in glove. They just want you to get your work done, and the sooner the better.

CHAPTER 3   SECRET #2: HIGHLY EFFECTIVE SOCIAL IMPACT COMMUNICATORS ...
            ARE ASTUTE TRANSLATORS INSIDE AND OUTSIDE OF THEIR ORGANIZATIONS

You and I can start to change that paradigm. We have already established why: to do your best work, you must study your toolbox of tools, better known as your personal values, and put them to work intentionally. You could probably pound a nail into a board with the butt end of a drill, but it would be a slow and painful process. The drill might break. It could bend the nail into uselessness.

So how can you line up the right value to the right solution?

Try writing out a short list of key solutions you provide. Then reference the list of key values you hold to be most important. Now, mix and match to see how they might line up to give your social impact communications an added boost.

Your list might end up looking something like this:

- **Writing → Conviction**
- **Editing → Compassion**
- **Facilitation/Leading → Stewardship**
- **Empowering → Nurture**
- **Building → Higher Calling**

Writing with **Conviction** gives your audience a sense of your expertise and the assurance you've done your homework. Conviction also gives you the courage to be open to changing your mind to make the best creative decisions in the moment. It pushes you forward to explore the vast spectrum of social impact stories available to you, not just a narrow band along that spectrum.

If you are **Editing**, then you are in a perfect position to demonstrate **Compassion.** This personal value applies to your subject matter just as much as it applies to your reader.

A common mistake I see often in social impact communication is its problematic word choice designed to make a group of people feel "less than." For example, in the world of food and agriculture where I come

CHAPTER 3   SECRET #2: HIGHLY EFFECTIVE SOCIAL IMPACT COMMUNICATORS ...
         ARE ASTUTE TRANSLATORS INSIDE AND OUTSIDE OF THEIR ORGANIZATIONS

from, many organizations elevate the small-farm owner who has a handful of animals and demean the large-farm owner who has hundreds or thousands of animals.

Social impact communicators don't put people down. They might disagree on how to solve a thorny problem like climate change. But then they recall farms of any size are run by people. They also employ people. People like you and me.

You catch more flies with honey than vinegar, as the saying goes. Editing with your values at the forefront brings stories to life for your audience. It also treats the people, issues, and stories you feature with kindness and care, no matter the position you or your organization hold on an issue.

You might not agree with everything your subject is doing. You might want to see things change—and more quickly, at that. The mark of a highly effective social impact communicator is to bring stories of environmental and social issues to the forefront so that *all* of us get something meaningful out of it. *All* of us can find some common ground somewhere.

If you are **Facilitating**, it makes sense to embrace the value of **Stewardship**. When you show genuine care for those around you, you serve them and the mission. Your colleagues' work directly impacts the social impact efforts of your organization.

When you have a busy day (which is to say, every day), it's tempting to cut conversations short, get cross with your team, and bury your head in your hands.

Resist the temptation to play by the lowest common denominator. Bring the care you feel for the cause directly to your team, your partners, and your communication. Guide people to be themselves and to show up at their finest, even in times of crisis. You never regret extending kindness, grace, and a family approach to your role. To steward the mission, you must first steward those around you.

CHAPTER 3   SECRET #2: HIGHLY EFFECTIVE SOCIAL IMPACT COMMUNICATORS ...
ARE ASTUTE TRANSLATORS INSIDE AND OUTSIDE OF THEIR ORGANIZATIONS

The solution of **Empowering** others means you get to apply the personal value of **Nurture**. I bet you've been on the receiving end of a parasitic relationship. Maybe someone stayed in contact with you not because they cared but because they knew you'd come to their rescue when things fell apart. You listened to their complaints and grievances.

You should do the opposite of that as a social impact communicator. You aren't here to make people feel bad or to complain. Instead, you are gifted in your ability to discern what people need. You know what they are good at. You meet their needs and help them play to their strengths. Look for ways to champion your team, far and wide. It's never been easier in a hybrid work environment to send a note, celebrate an accomplishment, or be there for someone going through a dark time. Your values will guide you to seek out these opportunities rather than stumbling upon them by accident.

Finally, your social impact communication role permits you to engage in **Building**. When you provide this solution, you apply the personal value of **Higher Calling**.

I'm guessing you don't do social impact work primarily for fame and fortune. (I won't fault you if those outcomes happen anyway.) I think you apply the best of your creativity, your research, and your intuition to make the world a better place. You see things others can't—at least not yet. You imagine worlds that haven't yet been fully formed. You're guided by principles beyond a vague aspiration of retiring in your mid-60s. You build for the long term. You're in this for the future of humanity.

You can connect the dots between your values and your solutions each day at work. I recommend pulling out your calendar for the upcoming week and taking a look at the activities you've planned. You might have a number of meetings, a couple of big-lift writing assignments, and some conversations with your team.

Don't think of these activities as boxes to check. Instead, see them for what they are: opportunities to bring your whole self to work, unapologetically, while you lead with your values.

CHAPTER 3   SECRET #2: HIGHLY EFFECTIVE SOCIAL IMPACT COMMUNICATORS ...
ARE ASTUTE TRANSLATORS INSIDE AND OUTSIDE OF THEIR ORGANIZATIONS

When you reframe your role as a person who empowers, who nurtures, and who demonstrates compassion, I am convinced you will feel better about yourself—and your colleagues will notice immediately. Done over and over again, this cultivates a habit of purpose, deeper meaning, and more sincere communication. It benefits everyone in your organization. It helps your partners and strengthens relationships. It brings greater authenticity and nuance to your external communications.

Above all, it will grow you personally into a social impact communicator with the right priorities. Your actions can build an irreversible culture. People want more of what you have, not less. People want to be part of a mission whose adherents live the values they preach.

Why you must keep adding values to your toolbox

Let's step out of the sunshine for a moment and into the workshop of your mind once more.

Some parts of the workshop are well lit; others are hidden in shadow. This is the part where I tell you the work is not yet done. There are more values you need to locate. It's part of a lifelong process of discovery about who you are and why you were put here to do the work you're doing.

As a young newspaper editor, I stood boldly on the First Amendment and dared anyone to infringe upon it. I covered topics that made people uncomfortable yet needed to be addressed. These days, I'm still staunchly pro-speech, yet I also recognize there are times when discretion in what I say—and how I say it—is essential.

Life is an exercise in finding your boundaries and periodically resetting them.

As you grow in your social impact communication career, you find new values and deep pools of meaning buried within you. These values might not jump out of the shadows, just as tools seldom leap off the wall

CHAPTER 3   SECRET #2: HIGHLY EFFECTIVE SOCIAL IMPACT COMMUNICATORS ...
             ARE ASTUTE TRANSLATORS INSIDE AND OUTSIDE OF THEIR ORGANIZATIONS

at you. (Unless your workshop is haunted, but that is the subject of an entirely different book.) Instead, these values might emerge slowly as new opportunities and challenges you couldn't anticipate unfold around you.

At other times, you might find that a value you hold no longer serves you.

Adopt a new value, modify the old one, or both. In all cases, keep moving forward. This work is too important to stall for long.

But what if you encounter a situation where your values could be compromised?

This brings us to an interesting predicament. Sure, sticking to your values sounds fantastic. It sounds like a place of greater joy and fulfillment.

But life isn't so clean cut. What happens when you face a situation in which you are tempted to compromise your values. What should you do?

I can't say for sure because I'm not you. Our standards on some issues might be fixed. On other points, you might be more flexible than I am, and vice versa.

Still, there are some basic principles you can apply to determine how to proceed when you face turbulence as a social impact communicator.

Imagine your organization has set a major target for drawing down greenhouse gas (GHG) emissions. Your company works hard on this mission for years. Yet on the eve of the big announcement—we've accomplished our GHG goal!—you learn something more complicated: your organization has not, in fact, achieved the target it intended.

Depending on your organization's required communications processes, a few options might stand before you. In the worst-case scenario, a supervisor might encourage you to fabricate a rosier picture or outright lie about the situation. I hope for your sake and mine that doesn't happen, though we increasingly hear charges that organizations

CHAPTER 3   SECRET #2: HIGHLY EFFECTIVE SOCIAL IMPACT COMMUNICATORS ... ARE ASTUTE TRANSLATORS INSIDE AND OUTSIDE OF THEIR ORGANIZATIONS

are greenwashing their way to a golden halo. In that type of scenario, you should find ways to advocate for the truth. Transparency trumps deceit every time.

A more realistic scenario is that your organization sets goals and falls short of them. This happens every day. It's normal. It isn't a case of compromised values but of predictable setbacks on a long and fruitful journey of social impact. You and I set goals because we want to accomplish big things and help other people. It's nearly impossible to guarantee those goals, so we instead rightly focus on the actions that help us get closer to them.

Your first reaction to a missed goal might be, "What a shame. Why couldn't my organization get its act together?"

Yet let's face the facts: organizations are led and built by individuals. You are one of them! There's no shame in missing a goal. Rather, a missed goal represents an opportunity for self-reflection and organizational reflection. This is what differentiates a highly effective social impact communicator from an aspiring changemaker who has little tolerance for organizational shortcomings.

You as a highly effective social impact communicator can make several important choices to productively move through a setback (much more on this later in the book). I recommend these:

- Choose to assume positive intent. If mistakes were made, they were honest ones, not Hollywood movie white-collar criminal ones.

- Avoid jumping to conclusions. You might have missed a goal, but what did you gain anyway?

- Take a step back and consider the circumstances. What factors influencing your leadership, your organization, or the wider market might have contributed to this outcome?

- Remind yourself of your and your organization's integrity. Think of all the times on this social impact journey that you and your organization applied wisdom, put your values to work, and worked toward the goal.

These mental choices equip you for conversations about how your organization can regroup and reset its goals—and then talk openly about where you are headed next.

Avoid making decisions on your own. Get feedback. Talk through scenarios. Imagine the audiences you are trying to reach. Treat one another and anyone who will touch your final communication with extreme respect and dignity. This is especially important if you face unpleasant news. You and your colleagues are under enough stress already, no fiery rhetoric required.

The words you choose matter less than the way you show up to craft the communication. Your treatment of the process and of one another matters most.

Embrace collaboration to reach a solution that makes everyone proud. This minimizes the risk of you or your organization compromising your values or becoming demoralized. Good, clear, and candid communication will carry you through, internally and externally.

Define your "actions accompanying values"—when X happens, I will do Y

The more you practice your response to events that could jeopardize your values, the better prepared you are to handle whatever comes your way.

Completing the following chart can help you plan far in advance of any potential problems.

CHAPTER 3   SECRET #2: HIGHLY EFFECTIVE SOCIAL IMPACT COMMUNICATORS ...
            ARE ASTUTE TRANSLATORS INSIDE AND OUTSIDE OF THEIR ORGANIZATIONS

The left-hand column features common scenarios social impact communicators might encounter on the job. You can add rows with other situations you've faced.

The right-hand column remains blank for you to fill in how you intend to respond if you face that event. It's helpful to envision these situations happening with people at different levels of your organization. Consider how you would respond if your CEO approached you compared to a peer or a member of your team. You should also think through how you would respond if a customer, client, or partner organization initiated the scenario.

Your answers are your own. The principles of personal values that we've discussed up to this point can guide you.

Scenario	Values-Driven Response
If I'm told we're going to miss a social impact goal ...	Then I will ...
If we make a mistake in our public social impact communications ...	Then I will ...
If a partner in our social impact work does something against our values ...	Then I will ...
If a social impact program in my portfolio loses funding ...	Then I will ...
If someone identifies something I've done or said in conflict with our social impact mission ...	Then I will ...

You can imagine potential scenarios and responses in your mind or, better yet, use this as a journaling exercise. Some of your gut reactions might surprise you.

Think through multiple potential paths you could take. Always leave yourself options. Social impact communications are too important and too complex to lean on simplistic responses to these situations.

CHAPTER 3   SECRET #2: HIGHLY EFFECTIVE SOCIAL IMPACT COMMUNICATORS ...
ARE ASTUTE TRANSLATORS INSIDE AND OUTSIDE OF THEIR ORGANIZATIONS

What to do when values conflict: Understand, align as possible, and influence

I haven't yet addressed perhaps the most likely culprit for conflict as you put your values to work: What if other people's values conflict with mine? What happens when we must work on a team with people who fundamentally don't share our values and worldview?

First, take pride in the talent and skill you've cultivated as a social impact communicator. There's a reason you've been assigned to this role. You're capable of handling even the most complex interpersonal dynamics—or calling in backup if needed.

Second, seek to understand. If you and a colleague disagree on a point, or team members are at odds, focus on questions and information gathering, rather than criticizing or deciding.

What exactly is at issue? What values do the people in the room hold? Which ones are in conflict, and why? How far apart are these individuals (or teams), really?

We humans have a funny way of blowing things out of proportion before we pause, take a deep breath, and seek to meet once again in the middle. (Ask me how I know.)

Avoid the temptation to be rash. You, more than most, understand the power of words. Apply your personal values. Keep yourself out of the emotional sawgrass. Seek to bring people together.

Third, focus on alignment. You'll never agree with everyone 100% of the time. At the same time, you must be willing to seek common ground to advance a social impact mission together with our fellow flawed humans.

See what you can do to bring alignment. Point your colleagues, teammates, or clients back to the mission at hand. Remind them individually of the contributions they've made to the success of the group. Remember what outcome you're striving for. Then, align in writing on the conditions you each must meet to move forward.

Maybe you agree to disagree. Maybe you distribute the work differently so each person can bring their strongest values to the table. Get outside help if needed. Focus on reaching compromises and solving problems all of you agree on.

Fully embrace your values and lead with them at every stage of the resolution process. Your influence matters. You've done the hard work of honing your values and discovering new ones. You have greater inner strength and outward calm to move forward.

Replace conflict with understanding. Accept responsibility and share praise. Move the mission forward with people who see in you both sincerity and shared commitment to the mission.

Learn to discover others' values quickly—and work toward them together

It's healthy to learn about the values your colleagues hold. You've probably taken personality tests and scored yourself three ways to Sunday. Some people are extroverts. Others are introverts. Many are both.

Yet we're way more nuanced than that. Unfortunately, our values too often get overlooked or subsumed into the sea of "What work must immediately be done today?"

Remind one another of your personal values and your organization's values. Set intentions or goals designed to help each person on your social impact team move closer to making those values a reality in their lives.

The closer we get to living out our values, the more skilled we become. We show up at work with those values. We bring a deep toolbox capable of helping those around us. We reach the ambitious social impact goals we've set, whether for our environment or in our communities.

CHAPTER 3   SECRET #2: HIGHLY EFFECTIVE SOCIAL IMPACT COMMUNICATORS ...
            ARE ASTUTE TRANSLATORS INSIDE AND OUTSIDE OF THEIR ORGANIZATIONS

Focus on the communications work itself, of course. But recognize the real exponential gains on your social impact journey happen when you invest in yourself and in the other people tasked with the mission.

Personal values aren't a fluffy marshmallow aspiration. They're the wrenches and vices and impact drivers that shape a better world.

Embrace a bigger worldview than you thought possible

By the time night falls on the workshop of your mind, you are probably exhausted and unsure what exactly happened that day. It happens to me all the time. When you are focused on the mission, time flies! But do you know something? You're now one step closer to perfecting the skill of knowing your values. You can define them and practice how to use them.

Chances are good you've helped others do the same with their values, too. It's painstaking work that requires care, practice, and occasionally smashing one's finger with the blunt end of a hammer. (Please not with the claw end. That would really hurt!)

When you turn off the lights in your workshop and close the door behind you, there will be a moment of breathless vertigo. Pay attention to what happens next: a calming sense of inner peace.

Why? You've brought your higher self to work. You and your colleagues have conducted a creative orchestra using social impact communications designed to do lasting good for the world.

You might not have done much today—at least, that you can see clearly. Yet the incremental investments you make pay off.

They make us better at our work.

They help us treat one another with greater love, kindness, and respect.

They build workplaces that prioritize people over products or profit.

CHAPTER 3   SECRET #2: HIGHLY EFFECTIVE SOCIAL IMPACT COMMUNICATORS ...
            ARE ASTUTE TRANSLATORS INSIDE AND OUTSIDE OF THEIR ORGANIZATIONS

That's what personal values and organizational values do for the circle of influence of a social impact communicator.

How do you build that circle of influence? How do you support a team doing things literally no one else in the history of the world has done? You embrace the renewable energy of teamwork. Let's see how in our next chapter.

Key Questions

- What person, movement, or legacy are you working to advance?

- Identify your top seven values and write them down. What made the cut, and why?

- Over which values are you most likely to experience conflict? How can you productively navigate this?

- When someone asks you to explain your motivation or drive for social impact work, what story do you tell?

- What value do you want others to see in you more than any other?

CHAPTER 4

Secret #4: Highly effective social impact communicators ... embrace the renewable fuel of teamwork

Everything I know about teamwork, I learned in high school. Well, that's not exactly accurate. But I did learn an awful lot about its incredible renewable properties as a member of *The South Paw*, the student newspaper at Niwot High School.

Let me say first—and this applies to everything I'll share with you in this book—that I've been blessed with the body, family, and circumstances that have informed my experiences. I don't take any of these privileges lightly. I hope my lived experience can inform your own purpose-driven journey, even though our experiences might be very different.

CHAPTER 4   SECRET #4: HIGHLY EFFECTIVE SOCIAL IMPACT COMMUNICATORS ... EMBRACE THE RENEWABLE FUEL OF TEAMWORK

My own experience with the power of teamwork began with my dad, who absolutely adored newspapers. On Sundays after worship services, dad found his way to the couch or a chair, a stack of newspapers next to him. As a student of history, an avid current events consumer, and a future librarian, dad loved catching up. He continues to clip stories and send them to his children today. It's a sign of love and care that still brings a smile to my face after all these years.

Next to my dad's chair lay *The Denver Post*, occasionally our local *Longmont Daily Times-Call*, and the *Rocky Mountain News*. Afterward, he'd come to the supper table with a fun fact or a cautionary tale or something in the news we needed to pay attention to.

I didn't understand it, at least at first. How could someone sit for hours with a piece of paper?

In high school, though, something sparked. I picked up a copy of the newspaper and discovered stories about ... how to choose the right makeup? This didn't make any sense. I applied to join the paper and noted the makeup exposé as an example of something I'd change.

The newspaper editors were warm and welcoming. They invited me over to their corner of the building for an interview and listened—perhaps even with a smile—as I shared my vision for the kinds of stories I'd contribute.

They gave me a shot, and it changed my career trajectory.

What I learned back then, and have seen over and over in my career supporting social impact programs across many organizations and industries, is that success in social impact communications can be engineered. It is not a perfect science, but there are strategies you can use to be effective through teamwork that is cohesive, holistic, and enthusiastic.

Research points us in this direction, particularly for complex tasks, which are part and parcel of purpose-driven work. As Duncan Watts, a professor at The Wharton School, has noted of a study he and his colleagues conducted:

CHAPTER 4 SECRET #4: HIGHLY EFFECTIVE SOCIAL IMPACT COMMUNICATORS … EMBRACE THE RENEWABLE FUEL OF TEAMWORK

Where teams really shine is in terms of efficiency. Teams for a complex task could do almost as well as the very best individual, but they were able to do it much quicker. That's because they were much faster, they generated more solutions, they generated faster solutions, and they explored the space of possibilities more broadly.[1]

My high school newspaper convened students from across the school, upperclassmen and greenies like me, to build something of interest to our peers. On publication days, which happened roughly six times each year, we'd show up before the crack of dawn and distribute the paper to each classroom. Between the excitement coursing through my body and the newsprint smearing my fingers, it was almost too much to bear. My pride for the work product we'd built together, and the anticipation of how the student body would react, drove me on.

From what I've seen working with clients on social impact issues, the only way to achieve incredible outcomes is for you as a communicator to contribute to a team culture that gets these results. When you learn how to turn a resource too often treated with extractive abandon into a resource that can be used and replenished again and again, the result is the renewable fuel of teamwork.

---

[1] "Are Teams Better Than Individuals at Getting Work Done?" Knowledge at Wharton Podcast. October 12, 2021. https://knowledge.wharton.upenn.edu/podcast/knowledge-at-wharton-podcast/are-teams-better-than-individuals-at-getting-work-done/

CHAPTER 4   SECRET #4: HIGHLY EFFECTIVE SOCIAL IMPACT COMMUNICATORS ...
           EMBRACE THE RENEWABLE FUEL OF TEAMWORK

Burnout is real in social impact communication, even though we're so focused on the mission we ignore it

Once, my brother, Chad, and some friends of ours attempted to hike Pikes Peak, a famous mountain practically in our backyard. We intended to meet a few other companions, but our schedules didn't line up. The four of us made the journey on our own.

We didn't have extensive experience hiking what are affectionately known as fourteeners—Colorado's peaks over 14,000 ft. in height. Instead, we had some water, some snacks, and the spirit of adventure.

Our hike began in the morning, and the rapidly climbing elevation became painfully obvious—quite literally. I could feel my legs gasping for oxygen with each passing step up and over the next big boulder.

At some point, we lost the trail and began making our way through the grass and what we thought might be a faint path cut by other former hikers. (When you get that high in elevation, your brain lacks oxygen. Your body isn't used to this sort of thing. You can imagine all kinds of things are real, even things thoroughly made up.)

It didn't end up being a trail. It was just a little path, probably made by other lost hikers, that led to the highway and completely took us away from the *actual* trail.

Providentially, the friends we'd intended to meet happened to drive by in their van as we reached the road. They picked us up as storm clouds gathered ominously overhead. Later that afternoon, we returned to our friends' home, ordered pizza, and collapsed. I've never slept as soundly as I did that afternoon, having come within striking range of the summit despite a technically unsuccessful outcome.

CHAPTER 4   SECRET #4: HIGHLY EFFECTIVE SOCIAL IMPACT COMMUNICATORS ... EMBRACE THE RENEWABLE FUEL OF TEAMWORK

This is what I call the good kind of burnout. Let's apply this to your work as a communicator. Your mission touches on social impact. You pour your heart and soul into the job. You jump from one meeting to another project to an emergency of some kind. Because you love the work and the people doing it alongside you, time passes and you don't regret it. You've left everything on the field, as we sometimes say here in the United States after a big sporting event.

There are many ways to do this. For example, you can invest that extra half hour in a project you truly believe in, rearranging your schedule so you get it right rather than fast. You can make the extra round of revisions because the people whose story you are telling can benefit. You can remain positive and optimistic in the face of unexpected challenges, choosing words that encourage your colleagues and remind them how you're making a positive difference in the world.

You're probably exhausted, but you wouldn't have it any other way. You tried to make a difference and succeeded because you worked together.

Now consider the opposite scenario. It plagues too many social impact professionals. You go to work focused primarily on growth and financial performance. You believe in showing appreciation but simply don't have a lot of extra bandwidth for it. Improving the quality of life for your team or tapping into the renewable fuel of teamwork feels like a task on an already long to-do list. Every day is a race in which the designated end point seems to move further away, well out of reach. You hop onto the hamster wheel every morning and hope to goodness someone pulls you off with a hook or a sharp yank before you collapse.

Does this sound familiar? Nearly eight in ten people report experiencing stress at work, according to an American Psychological Association (APA) study.[2]

---

[2] "The American workforce faces compounding pressure." American Psychological Association. 2021. www.apa.org/pubs/reports/work-well-being/compounding-pressure-2021

CHAPTER 4 SECRET #4: HIGHLY EFFECTIVE SOCIAL IMPACT COMMUNICATORS ...
         EMBRACE THE RENEWABLE FUEL OF TEAMWORK

I'm not a psychologist or a human resources expert. I won't claim to have the top life hack for alleviating your stress or that of your colleagues. But having worked across multiple industries as a communications professional and consultant, I've observed what makes social impact teams struggle. And I've also seen some common practices that help them stick with the mission and accelerate their progress.

I'm going to share those observations with you. I am hopeful that you, too, can tap into the renewable fuel of teamwork. It's the difference between having a good week and having a game-changing week. I bet you're even doing some of these things already without realizing it.

The thing is we need more game-changers. We need you and your team at your absolute best. We're all on deadline. I'll teach you how to beat the clock with less stress and more fulfilment. If you enjoy being grouchy and frowning a lot, maybe skip this chapter. Otherwise, keep reading. We're about to examine the attributes of the world's unhappiest teams. Then, I'll explain what highly effective social impact communicators do differently to take their teams to the moon.

Strategies for strengthening your social impact team by reversing the status quo

Unless you sit behind a mahogany desk with tented fingers plotting your team's certain doom, this section probably feels a little silly. Why in the world would anyone want a downtrodden team?

Yet it happens every day. If you aren't intentional about building a social impact team whose culture is vibrant and lively and encouraging, you'll reap a team that's stressed to the max, overworked, and underappreciated. Here are some warning signs that you're headed in the wrong direction:

CHAPTER 4   SECRET #4: HIGHLY EFFECTIVE SOCIAL IMPACT COMMUNICATORS ... EMBRACE THE RENEWABLE FUEL OF TEAMWORK

- You get so excited about the mission that you keep bringing together people in meetings to encourage one another and make decisions—eventually leading to meeting overwhelm.

- You get caught up in your own vision and establish your own personal theories and priority projects without considering that others' priorities—and the needs of your social impact mission—might differ from what you personally wish to see.

- You set ambitious deadlines because you recognize the seriousness of the work we're doing. Why wait when you could get after it?

- You focus on changing massive systems while downplaying the real potential to make a difference in just one other person's life.

- You celebrate the data while overlooking the stories of impact you and your team are having.

You don't have to work like that. I know you want to do better. You're actively pursuing something greater.

But what does that greater way look like? I'll show you. Here are several examples of what the status quo looks like—followed by choices you can make to model the most hopeful and energized social impact teams.

CHAPTER 4   SECRET #4: HIGHLY EFFECTIVE SOCIAL IMPACT COMMUNICATORS ... EMBRACE THE RENEWABLE FUEL OF TEAMWORK

Status quo: Conduct meetings that crush the soul

Have you ever participated in meetings with no clear purpose and with the frenzy of a Tasmanian devil? Me too. Michael Hyatt's book *No Fail Meetings*[3] is a great resource for you and your colleagues to study. The best meetings help us gain clarity, reach consensus, make decisions, and move forward on social impact projects. The worst meetings find us all agreeing when secretly we don't, or talking ourselves in circles, or making short-term decisions with long-term repercussions we haven't considered. Treat yourself and your colleagues with enough respect to hold meetings on purpose, rather than on hostage. This looks like having an agenda and following it. It also means asking questions that invite your team into conversation and curiosity, rather than delivering mandates and opinions.

Your choice: Conduct meetings that embolden and launch

For you to be most effective as a social impact communicator, you must help organize meetings that embolden yourself and your colleagues for excellence in everything you do. Your goal is never to have a meeting for the sake of a meeting. It's to create a launch pad for the next phase of growth and impact. It's to brainstorm opportunities to help your customers or partners or society.

---

[3] "No Fail Meetings: 5 Steps to Orchestrate Productive Meetings (and Avoid all the Rest)." Michael Hyatt. Jan. 1, 2018. www.amazon.com/No-Fail-Meetings-Orchestrate-Productive/dp/1732189633/ref=sr_1_3?crid=3DMEYE639XYKC&keywords=no+fail+meetings+michael+hyatt&qid=1685444616&sprefix=no+fail+meetings%2Caps%2C179&sr=8-3

CHAPTER 4   SECRET #4: HIGHLY EFFECTIVE SOCIAL IMPACT COMMUNICATORS ... EMBRACE THE RENEWABLE FUEL OF TEAMWORK

Status quo: Cast a vision only you can see

All of us have hopes and dreams. But sometimes, those dreams become toxic when we pursue them despite information to the contrary. Sad and depleted teams frequently are at the mercy of a well-intentioned leader so convinced of the moral good they're doing that they forget to act like an adult human being. Instead, they can be careless, rude, persistently stubborn in the face of new information, and so on.

Great social impact leaders cast a vision their team can believe in. They solicit feedback. They ask about blind spots they might have overlooked. Then, the leader makes a decision, though it's more of a collaborative effort than a mandate.

Your choice: Co-create your vision with your team

Bring people together and get their best ideas before committing to a plan of action. Reserve your opinions and philosophies for times of quiet reflection. Don't turn half-baked ideas into mandates your team must act upon. Find ways to co-create programs, solutions, and communications activities that make you all proud. After all: You will have built these things together to meet a need in the marketplace, your community, or both. Avoid the temptation to tell people how it's going to be. Decide how it's going to be together.

Status quo: Set deadlines impossible from the word "go"

The planning fallacy[4] is a cognitive bias that prevents us from accurately predicting how long a task will take. Apply this to social impact settings and the results can be disastrous. For example, you or someone you

---

[4] "Why do we underestimate how long it will take to complete a task?" The Decision Lab. https://thedecisionlab.com/biases/planning-fallacy

follow might set an overly ambitious timeframe for completing a big grant proposal. Or perhaps you're trying to start up a new public-private partnership and want to do so by Thursday. These kinds of pursuits, while exciting and adrenaline pumping, ignore the slow and steady crockpot approach often necessary. Building relationships, cultivating trust, and finding common ground inside and outside of your organization require a substantial investment of time you must prioritize, however unpopular.

Your choice: Set realistic and flexible deadlines

When it's done well, social impact work is inspiring and meaningful. Yet it requires the discipline of a marathon runner, not a sprinter. A better analogy might be that of driving through a construction zone on the highway. You know you're going to reach your final destination because you're moving carefully and deliberately. You're watching out for traffic cones and paused cars. You're remaining conscious of your surroundings and preparing to take a detour when necessary. But you will get there. Because you and your team are realistic and flexible.

Status quo: Treat people like commodities— all alike

The "go big or go home" philosophy can pervade social impact work. And why not? It's already a big driver in most other lines of work. End global climate change now! Make the world more equitable for mankind right away! Yet focusing only on this giant outcome can be damaging for you and your team. You don't build widgets on an assembly line, as we've already discussed. Yet you might be tempted to go for broke on those big goals of helping every single human. This can cause us to lose sight of the individual traits that make us special as human beings. You have personalized choice and feelings. You know what really matters in life. Why wouldn't your fellow human beings? The risk you and I inadvertently treat our fellow man like a commodity easily manipulated and sold to is real. Don't do it.

Your choice: Put people first, work together, and make something great

You are enthusiastic about permanently changing the status quo. That's admirable. There's always room to grow. Don't lose sight of the fact that systems change one person at a time. A communications campaign you launch today might be the motivator for a lawmaker or a farmer or a banker or another leader to make decisions that improve the lives of thousands or millions of people. It starts small, one by one. Like grains of sand in a sand castle, we can come together as individual human beings and make something amazing. Don't lose sight of the individual contributors in your team and in your audience who are part of your social impact mission. They can take your efforts and multiply them.

Status quo: Celebrate statistics only, not accompanying success stories

I love a good research study for the insights it can reveal and the things it can teach us. Yet I'm also aware data can become a tool that mirrors back to us whatever we want to see. This includes preexisting views about how the world works. You and I run the risk of focusing on data and statistics tied to our social impact work—so much so that we ignore opportunities to hear directly from the people we're trying to help in their own words. We might even ignore those with whom we partner on social impact work. As a professional communicator, it's important to remember that we're doing heart work and head work. Cultivate a team that looks for opportunities to seek out human stories and bring them to the collective attention.

Appreciate data and outcomes for the insights and direction they provide. Treat it as a tool in your toolbox. The potential of people's stories to inspire and motivate us to action on social impact issues shouldn't be overlooked.

Your choice: Celebrate stories of impact underpinned by data

Data points show change on a broader scale and aren't exciting on their own, at least to a grizzled old communicator like me. Instead, they're a reflection of the people whose lives you are changing. They show change on a broader scale. They demonstrate how people's decisions and worldviews are trending. When you and your team celebrate the impact you're having, focus first on the lives you're changing. Think back to times in your life when you've made monumental decisions: you reached a crossroads and chose to change. That same feeling is what you're creating for your audience and the wider world: the chance to make a change at the crossroads. The chance to transform society for the better. As a social impact communicator, you're privileged to create meaningful connections with individuals and benefits that extend beyond them. You have the power. Your work matters.

How to foster a mindful and impactful team using the PURSUE framework

The tactics I've just described have repeatedly help me tap into the renewable energy of teamwork as a social impact communicator.

But if you simply apply them at random, you won't successfully tackle the biggest, gnarliest problems your team faces. In fact, you might end up flailing around while your most ambitious social impact goals go unmet.

CHAPTER 4 SECRET #4: HIGHLY EFFECTIVE SOCIAL IMPACT COMMUNICATORS ... EMBRACE THE RENEWABLE FUEL OF TEAMWORK

What you need to effectively leverage the renewable energy of teamwork is a strategic framework. Something that pulls all of these concepts together into a bucket or a basket. A plan of action that helps you understand, "If I do this, then that happens." People aren't predictable like machines, but we often behave in ways that can be anticipated.

I've worked with dozens of clients across different industries and social impact projects. Through those experiences, I've discovered that the best teams embrace the following framework to get more meaningful work done. What's more, they're able to walk away whole at the end of the day—their values and personal lives firmly intact.

I call it the PURSUE framework. Let's examine each element together, and I think you will see how it simplifies the process of turning your team into an incredible source of renewable energy.

Positive

The right attitude is the difference between slogging through a day with dozens of tasks on your plate and skipping through your day recognizing each activity puts you one step closer to the change you want to make. Embrace the spirit of optimism and joy even on the most challenging days. A positive attitude is infectious in the best possible way.

Understandable

Great teams work together to get clear on their vision, mission, needs, and deadlines—internally and externally. If you hope to get something meaningful done, you must be unified in the knowledge of what you are doing and how you relay those goals to others. I've watched too many high potential professionals run in place because they couldn't get traction explaining their mission, articulating what help they needed, or both. Teams generating tons of renewable energy study one another's strengths and weaknesses. They play to their strengths. They collaborate to compensate for the weak points.

Relatable

As Solomon wrote in the Bible's Book of Proverbs, "A man who has friends must himself be friendly."[5] Chances are good that no matter the size or age of your organization, you work with other human beings in some capacity. It might be with other divisions in your business, nonprofit, or government agency. It might be outside partners or funders. It could even be with the audiences your communications serve. In all of these cases, being relatable, approachable, and easy to work with is essential. Your ego might drive you to build and deliver a new product, service, or project, which is great—we need your contributions. (Remember my early days at the high school newspaper? Ego and I were besties.) Yet ego has its limitations. Once it gets you started, it's time for other cooler heads to prevail. Step back and let us see the amazing contributions of that team that made your co-created vision come to life. Be approachable, humble, and generous. Which is to say, be relatable.

Stalwart

The slow and steady work of social impact demands you be consistent and dependable, even under adverse circumstances. It's possible to launch a consumer product, make some fast money, and walk away happy and rich. But social impact activities tend to require ample research, gradual entry into the marketplace, study of outcomes, and ongoing fine-tuning. No one expects you to have everything figured out, nice as that would be. Your team must have the fortitude to keep going on the bright days and the rainy ones, during setbacks and mountaintop experiences. Be an adaptable rock and prepare to adjust if needed. But be a rock nonetheless.

---

[5] Proverbs 18:24 (NKJV)

Useful

There's a place for research firms, think tanks, and policy organizations. The best social impact teams recognize the value of these groups and also aim to build on their contributions in a multidisciplinary, iterative way. They are committed to making their work practical and immediately useful in the world. You want to see measurable change in the world. You hope to see people engage more deeply on the most pressing challenges your generation faces. You always ask, "How can we make our work, and the communications we deliver about it, more useful?" You are endlessly resourceful. You high-five your team each time you offer something to the world that helps people live more sustainable lives, whatever the scale. And you are useful at a personal level, to your team and your partners in the social impact mission. You have your team's back. You take every opportunity to boost their morale and encourage them on the next project.

Enthusiastic

The best social impact teams acknowledge the privilege of getting to invest each day in work that's more meaningful than a product or a paycheck. They care deeply about the mission. They feel its glow within them. They cherish each conversation with colleagues and each collaboration with partners. These activities generate new insights and the renewable energy to keep learning, leading, and communicating.

Because you've chosen the path of a highly effective social impact communicator, you can now help your team embrace and follow the PURSUE framework. Chances are pretty good that your team already has several of these attributes in spades.

If you and your colleagues already do many of these things, great! Keep going. Practice will help you improve at applying these attributes in different circumstances. This framework can get you through great times and challenging ones.

CHAPTER 4   SECRET #4: HIGHLY EFFECTIVE SOCIAL IMPACT COMMUNICATORS ...
             EMBRACE THE RENEWABLE FUEL OF TEAMWORK

PURSUE depth of relationship and compassionate collaboration. PURSUE an approach to teamwork that will be the envy of other social impact teams. PURSUE sharing knowledge.

What are you learning about what it takes to be an incredibly effective and generous social impact team? I want to learn from you. (You can email me with your experiences at nate@silvermaplestrategies.com—I respond personally to each message.) I bet your colleagues in your chosen industry want to learn from you, too!

If you see one or more gaps in how you or your team shows up, don't worry. I see those same gaps in myself. You're normal.

Bring your team together—remember, social impact communication requires you to pair your technical abilities as a communicator with leadership—and walk through this framework together. Select just one area to start cultivating more deeply. What did you land on, and why? Talk through each person's perspective on what benefits could derive from dedicated focus to that area.

Perhaps you decide to collectively focus on R for Relatable. What could your team gain from operating at its friendliest and most approachable? What could you learn from approachable peers or partner organizations? The potential is limitless. For example, streamlining and improving relationships might enable you to make decisions faster, get projects completed sooner, or expand your service offering more rapidly.

Spend time brainstorming your dedicated area of focus. Then predict potential benefits. Identify three to five action steps you'll take to put the concept into practice. For example, a team focused on relatability might choose to

- Show up to meetings at least five minutes early, demonstrating respect and care for colleagues.

- Follow up on delivering what you've promised, whether it's a follow-up email or a communications campaign launched by a certain due date.

- Ask your colleagues and partners how their lives are going and how their families are doing, without prompting. Show you care before you show what you're capable of doing as a communicator.

- Listen twice as often as you talk. Take good notes you can use to guide future collaboration with others.

- Share at least one positive thing you've learned about a colleague or partner to break the ice at the start of meetings. Practice transferring knowledge and empathy so you're all at your best for those with whom you work.

Your list might look even more specific than this one. Or you might start more broadly and simply focus on recognizing opportunities throughout your day to practice being relatable and approachable.

Put the PURSUE framework into action. You'll immediately begin reaping the benefits of greater compassion, empathy, and productivity.

When the going gets tough, turn to daily micro habits to get unstuck and get going

Maybe all this warm and fuzzy stuff sounds about as appealing as winning an oversized teddy bear at a carnival. It's kind of cute, but it makes no sense to you. Can't we be a bit more specific and practical for a moment?

Yes we can. And it's where we're going right now.

I share the PURSUE framework not because I want you to embrace fuzzy feelings with religious fervor. Instead, I am coaching you so you have the skills needed to thrive as a social impact communicator. I've seen too many teams fester and lose traction through dysfunction.

CHAPTER 4 SECRET #4: HIGHLY EFFECTIVE SOCIAL IMPACT COMMUNICATORS ... EMBRACE THE RENEWABLE FUEL OF TEAMWORK

A common scenario looks like this: Team Member A isn't perceived as pulling their weight (and genuinely, they might not work as hard as others). Your leader comes to you and says, "Please work with Team Member A. Give them clear direction on what we need them to be doing and by when. Help them understand the consequences of failing to get up to speed."

You have a polite yet awkward conversation with Team Member A about their actions at work and the need for change. They express surprise and vow to do better.

In some cases, you notice small yet positive changes right away. In other cases, the behavior in question continues along with a distinct feeling of resentment. Now you have all the ingredients of a toxic soup. Your colleague feels confused and betrayed. Your leader wants you to double down on corrective action. You don't know which way to turn first. You just want to get back to the social impact communication you're committed to delivering.

It might be that this is a human resources issue you ignored or failed to recognize sooner. Or it might be that the stress, complexity, and relentless pace of social impact work are clouding your vision, at least a bit.

There is a way to get help, and quickly. Micro habits, when practiced across your entire team, fuel a sense of purpose and mission and collaborative care that fits beautifully into the PURSUE framework. You don't have to be Peter Drucker or another management genius to apply them. Nor do you need to have the bedside manner of a clergy or the listening abilities of a therapist.

You simply need to show up, be yourself without apology, and recognize that the micro habits you implement either add energy to you and your team or deplete it. And more energy for everyone means more opportunities to get closer to making good on the mission.

It isn't someone else's job to figure out how to nurture a winning social impact team. As a communicator, that's on you. Read the book *Extreme Ownership* by Jocko Willink and Leif Babin. The sooner you step up for your colleagues, the faster you get to enjoy the results of accountability and action.

Let's not dwell on theory. Let's explore some easy micro habits you and anyone on your team can use to make each day a little happier, more productive, and more encouraging. Remember, you're not in the teardown business. You're in the business of making a difference for your colleagues, your partners, and our world.

Let's do this!

Micro Habit #1: Great teams embrace the work and one another, flaws and all

When you dive into a social impact mission, how do you do it? Do you dip your toe in the water, test conditions, and hope things warm up to your liking? Or do you dive right in and get to work, ready to take on whatever opportunities or challenges come your way?

If you're like me, you take Option B every time. You dive straight in.

For some professions, that might be a mistake. You wouldn't build a house, for example, without a blueprint. You wouldn't want to start hammering sheetrock together (if you even use a hammer on sheetrock?) or laying roofing material onto thin air. You'd have a carefully laid-out plan built to the specifications you need.

I'm not suggesting you go into your work as a social impact communicator with zero plans. What I'm suggesting is that often in social impact work, you are

- Building the blueprint and building the house at the same time

- Calling audibles and shifting approaches as new information arrives by the day

- Testing best practices for talking about and leading social impact work without an existing model to fall back on

This innovate-as-we-go approach might drive some people crazy, but I bet you get a thrill out of it. What could be more fun than finding new ways to help people, strengthen our environment, and foster greater equity?

You embrace the work not only for its potential benefits but for the process itself. You surround yourself with a team of fellow human beings who, while flawed, are as committed as you are to the mission and the daily discipline of learning and growing.

Yes, this includes flaws, biases, and occasional bullheadedness. You recognize that in time, your relationships strengthen, your perspective softens, and you become someone capable of greater effectiveness in your work, greater nuance in your decision-making, and greater skill in the art of social impact communication.

You embrace the work because of what it generates and what you become in the process.

Micro Habit #2: Great teams overpower the isolation and misunderstood nature of social impact work

Imagine you are an okapi living in the forest. You are something of a mystery: Your back side is all zebra, and your upper body is something of a mashup between a horse and a rhinoceros.

Where exactly do you fit into the grand scheme of things, anyway? You might have felt the same way as a social impact communicator. Often, you sit somewhere between marketing and communications, between sustainability and human resources. You might report to two supervisors or be responsible for a bevy of duties that span multiple divisions. Whatever isolation you might feel personally, you don't have to feel alone. Chances are good that if your organization is invested in social impact—or moving in that direction—there are leaders and peers in your corner.

CHAPTER 4   SECRET #4: HIGHLY EFFECTIVE SOCIAL IMPACT COMMUNICATORS ... EMBRACE THE RENEWABLE FUEL OF TEAMWORK

In the consulting work I've done across multiple organizations, there's almost always a cohort of two or more people figuring this out together.

They bounce ideas off of one another. They face each setback with curiosity. When a test doesn't go as expected, they try to figure out what happened and how to do things differently in the future. They tag-team efforts. They leave the safety of their office, conduct research, ask questions, formulate hypotheses, and experiment with new methods for social impact communication and building social impact programs.

They're active learners.

It's easy to feel misunderstood when your organization is still finding its sea legs on social impact. Even after your organization commits and starts building out a more structured plan, you might still feel pulled in multiple directions. That's normal, and it's also healthy. Better to be pulling in the same direction than to be pulled apart trying to get off the launch pad.

Learn to recognize the body language of your colleagues who are feeling stressed, overwhelmed, or confused. Reassure them you're in this together. Look for opportunities to say a kind word. Ask questions about how they're doing and see what they might need you to help with. The most effective social impact communicators take charge even if they don't hold an executive title. They recognize their best work happens in community. They depend on creative feedback and clever ideas shared by multiple people, not just ideas they whipped up on their morning walk.

Build a sense of community by asking others for feedback. Share your original ideas. Create something brand new as your individual perspectives coalesce.

CHAPTER 4   SECRET #4: HIGHLY EFFECTIVE SOCIAL IMPACT COMMUNICATORS ...
            EMBRACE THE RENEWABLE FUEL OF TEAMWORK

Micro Habit #3: Great teams know one another personally as well as professionally

I've always found it funny that some organizations go to great lengths to build a tall wall between employees' personal lives and their professional careers. Sometimes, we get so focused on tracking hours, monitoring performance, and churning out high-quality deliverables that we lose sight of the fact we're humans with lives and interests outside of work.

If we paid even a little more attention to our own experiences, thoughts, and feelings—and those of our peers—maybe our work would be even richer and more meaningful to the people we're working to serve.

Everyone approaches this micro habit a bit differently. But in my experience, great teams doing social impact communications work take the time to build friendships grounded in mutual respect and familial care for their peers.

I'm not suggesting you unlock the doors to your home and host barbecues or five-course dinners every Friday. (If that's your thing, great! Please send me an invitation, as I'm free next Friday.)

Instead, you can take smaller steps that have a positive influence on your colleagues. Keep tabs of your team members' birthdays. Learn what drives their passion for the social impact work you're doing together. Did something happen in childhood that sparked a fascination with the natural world, maybe wildlife habitat specifically? Are they working toward a big personal goal such as publishing a book or buying a home? Are they setting up their children for success after high school graduation?

People are fascinating and complex, just as social impact work is fascinating and complex. None of us exists in a vacuum. Your effectiveness as a social impact communicator depends on your ability to appreciate how each piece of the puzzle that is your team works together. Together, you are building something greater than any one person could accomplish.

CHAPTER 4   SECRET #4: HIGHLY EFFECTIVE SOCIAL IMPACT COMMUNICATORS ... EMBRACE THE RENEWABLE FUEL OF TEAMWORK

As Helen Keller is reported to have said, "I would rather walk with a friend in the dark than alone in the light."

This kind of compassionate collaboration is especially important in an increasingly polarized world. Social media and generative AI, among other tools, have made it easy to build and deliver any message or content with lightning speed. Yet our personal relationships can't survive such volatility. We must get to know one another more deeply, on our best days and our darkest, to weather the inevitable highs and lows of social impact work.

One day, the media or other outside observers might be in your corner, explaining how your social impact mission is essential and revolutionizing the world. The next day, you might be painted as a has-been—worse yet, as a tool of damage and destruction for society.

Grow deeply rooted convictions, and seek to understand and appreciate the deep convictions of your colleagues. Encourage one another in the work. Peer into the deep wells of your lives that contain your values and your sense of purpose and duty.

These daily practices will give you the resolve you need to keep going, arm in arm.

Micro Habit #4: Great teams draw energy from complementary capabilities

In addition to appreciating the personal lives of your team, it's also important that you understand the unique professional capabilities they bring to the work of social impact communications. Chances are good the skills you've cultivated are different than the skills your peers have cultivated. Together, you can piece together something incredible.

I have observed great social impact communicators engaged in a bit of a verbal relay race to make this most effective.

CHAPTER 4 SECRET #4: HIGHLY EFFECTIVE SOCIAL IMPACT COMMUNICATORS ... EMBRACE THE RENEWABLE FUEL OF TEAMWORK

Here's how it works: Suppose you're on deadline for a big communications campaign. You are a pro writer, fast and clear, with minimal errors. Your colleague is a crack editor and catches any subtle imperfection in your writing.

Over a quick video call or a chat thread, you divvy up the work. You'll do the writing, and your colleague will edit. You verbally commit to one another as to the time and date on which you'll deliver your piece of the work. You talk through contingencies—if I get delayed, then I will ask for help. Or: If the sources I am attempting to interview fall through, then we will reconvene and brainstorm three more people to participate in this project.

The secret sauce is in the call and response. I learned this from a leader I admire deeply, and it works like a charm. You affirm what you will do, and you listen as the other person acknowledges what you have said. Now you have a compact.

When you bring your two skill sets together, you complement one another and produce an outstanding final product. You bring unique perspectives to social impact communications. You turn your original viewpoint into the craft of writing, or editing, or design, or leadership, or any other task.

This provides energy for several reasons. First, it ensures you're only doing work that is your highest and best use. Second, you're not wasting energy grinding away at a task you're not excellent at. Third, you're gaining confidence performing at your highest level in a state of flow. You're doing the work you love and honing your already-excellent skill set.

Fourth, you're drawing inspiration from watching your colleagues do what they do best. This promotes a fifth benefit, which is learning more about how social impact communications can best be performed. You're observing how best to work with your team to get the results you all want.

Great teams draw energy from one another because they put the right people on the right tasks. Collectively, they build something amazing. You can build amazing things every day as a social impact communicator, even if it's merely the foundation for something greater on the horizon.

Micro Habit #5: Great teams show gratitude before attitude—there's nothing to prove until you have something to prove

I've watched several social impact teams stutter, stop, and stutter again. It's not because they lacked a compelling vision for making our environment healthier. It's not because they failed to set goals for making the world better.

Instead, they fell short because they held onto an ancient enemy: ego. Rather than working collectively, they worked unilaterally. This is often, but not exclusively, the result of an ambitious leader who thinks they have all the answers.

These leaders tend to be insecure, in that they're unwilling—or afraid—to hear differing perspectives. They don't stop long enough to appreciate the hard work happening by their team on the front lines. They insist on pursuing their plan of action in spite of evidence suggesting another approach could be more effective.

In the worst cases, ego-driven leaders demean their colleagues, press them for unreasonable volumes of work, and never express gratitude. Their cup is perpetually empty. They demand never-ending refills. This type of behavior is the single-use plastic of leadership: endless in its wastefulness and negligent of the collateral damage stacking up beneath its heavy weight.

You won't do that sort of thing because you're a highly effective social impact communicator. Instead, you'll choose to show gratitude. And when you achieve those big goals you've written on your whiteboard, you'll give credit where it's due—to the hardworking people surrounding you.

The fun thing about gratitude is that it opens up space for new opportunities to do more good in the future. You aren't entitled to these opportunities. You've earned the privilege because you and your team showed up. You saw a need. You worked hard to address it. You listened closely and adapted your communications strategy. You stayed the course.

Great team members aren't so vain as to believe they hung the moon. Instead, they stay humble and embrace gratitude as an expression of the real magic—teamwork and collaboration.

Micro Habit #6: Great teams navigate complexity with calm, not chaos

There's a fun book capable of giving you a good shot of adrenaline called *It Doesn't Have to Be Crazy at Work.* Written by the founders of Basecamp software, it shares some of the organization's founding principles. Many of them focus on resisting the temptation to race around at work as if you were responding to a three-alarm fire.

I've spent a lot of my career at the intersection of agriculture and climate change, and I know there's plenty I could worry about: falling water levels. Rising temperatures. Changing seasons. Shifting wildlife habitats.

It would be understandable to express alarm.

If the desire to address these things gets you up in the morning, great. I hope you'll stay motivated to go out and do a great job. But the reality in too many cases is that emphasizing anxiety breeds chaos. This risks rash decision-making and treating team members as expendable objects on a quest for impossibly big goals on absurdly small time horizons.

CHAPTER 4 SECRET #4: HIGHLY EFFECTIVE SOCIAL IMPACT COMMUNICATORS ... EMBRACE THE RENEWABLE FUEL OF TEAMWORK

For the social impact communicator, chaos looks like

- Juggling multiple campaigns
- Developing and launching a partnership program
- Building communications assets to keep filling your organization's pipeline with new clients in need of help

Those activities in and of themselves are wonderful! The challenge becomes: With so many competing demands, at what point do you sacrifice your humanity? When do you trade your capacity to treat others with kindness and respect for a churn-and-burn, build-the-empire-at-any-expense approach?

If you or your colleagues are tempted to set aside calm in favor of chaos, remember that both are mindsets. You can choose which to embrace and reflect in your workplace. For example:

- If your supervisor schedules a last-minute meeting and asks for all hands on deck, be willing to push pause on other projects to respond to that need. If your social impact leader is attuned to the marketplace and to the needs of your organization, they probably have a good reason for seeking immediate attention.
- If a project ends up taking twice as long as you expected, pull your colleagues together and explore which puzzle pieces within your division can be rearranged to accommodate the time and attention this lengthy project deserves.

The two things that disappear most quickly when chaos rears its ugly head are (1) personal sanity and (2) the quality of the work you're doing. Don't compromise either.

Take a few deep breaths. Remember, you're doing multigenerational work (more on that toward the end of this book). Recall you're on a team of people ready, willing, and able to help you get through to the other side.

Exude calm and your peers follow.

Micro Habit #7: Great teams seek cohesion rather than full clarity—people feel part of something great, even external partners

Some assignments you tackle at work are spelled out in crystal clear detail. Like ice cubes in a transparent glass, you can see right to the heart of them. You can study each detail on its own merits.

In other cases, you're handed an assignment described in just two sentences. It's up to you to figure out what you need to know. You must determine how to solve the problem. You must decide who you need at the table to get this social impact communication work done.

Once, a leader I served shared we needed to apply for a major federal funding opportunity. My colleagues and I were intrigued yet recognized the heavy lifting and hurdles it could pose. We explained why we didn't feel it was the right time. Our supervisor remained stalwart (see the preceding text) in their conviction we needed to move forward.

No one stepped forward to claim the mission. I agreed to do whatever small part I could to move the project forward.

To figure out what I needed to do—because there wasn't a road map—I held a lot of meetings and phone calls with potential partners. I spent time at my desk brainstorming what we might accomplish together. I co-created with a large team of internal and external leaders a plan that, upon submission, earned us the chance to pursue a multimillion-dollar social impact program of work.

Along the way, I learned I wasn't alone. We all were feeling our way through this process for the first time. But what we lacked in clarity we made up for in cohesion.

We worked through possible scenarios. We debated budget line items. We imagined how we'd respond to the specific requirements of this award. We held the project up to the light and turned it around and upside down to see what we might be missing. This fostered a sense of unity.

You can do the same in your organization. You never have all the answers, but what you do have—especially as you apply the secrets shared in this book—is the ability to communicate with clarity and conviction. People watch what you do because it's clear you care. You know what you're about. You're prepared to make a difference that's bigger and bolder than any one person.

You have the ability to convene and to make people feel included as valued contributors to the cause.

Micro Habit #8: Great teams champion honesty, admit when things could be better, and work to make it so

This might come as a shock to you, but not all social impact activities are fun. Depending on your industry and your reporting requirements, there are aspects of this work that can feel like what Full Focus founder Michael Hyatt in his book *Free To Focus* calls drudgery.

For you, workplace misery might look like completing progress reports, or analyzing large databases, or conducting high-stakes wrap-up meetings in which you relive each aspect of a major program of work.

Sometimes, you'll have a great week or month but a rough day. Things don't go well. A partner expresses how upset they are that you made a certain decision. A project you felt was on solid ground starts to unwind.

CHAPTER 4   SECRET #4: HIGHLY EFFECTIVE SOCIAL IMPACT COMMUNICATORS ...
              EMBRACE THE RENEWABLE FUEL OF TEAMWORK

Rather than throwing up your hands at these moments, the most effective teams of social impact communicators openly admit when things aren't working. They sit with it.

I'm not talking about endless complaining and catastrophizing. I'm talking about accepting the facts for what they are. You talk out loud about what's great, what's not great, and what might be done, together as a team. Your goal is to ensure everyone comes through the storm without wanting to run screaming from the room.

Sometimes, these conversations are important but not urgent. You might have several weeks to consider options, conduct research, and make a decision.

In these cases, take as much time as you need. Remember, social impact will outlast us by design. There's no defined point of arrival. There are always opportunities to do better and help more people.

As such, the more strategy you apply to problems that crop up, the better positioned your team will be to make a lasting difference for years to come. Rushing often has the opposite effect. A fast solution might work for a short time, only to backfire later.

By contrast, you face important *and* urgent situations, too. Some decisions must be made rapidly—to repair a relationship or to get a project back on track, for example. In those cases, reference Micro Habit #5. Embrace calm.

Read *You're It* and related books, which illustrate how great leaders function in times of crisis. Bad things have a way of bringing us together. They expose a situation with all its flaws and shortcomings. And in that unity, that cohesion, you can work together to make circumstances bearable, if not better.

You can encourage one another. You can remind yourselves why you're doing this work. You can recall times you've overcome adversity in the past. Remind yourselves you've got this. Then get to work making it so.

CHAPTER 4   SECRET #4: HIGHLY EFFECTIVE SOCIAL IMPACT COMMUNICATORS ... EMBRACE THE RENEWABLE FUEL OF TEAMWORK

Teamwork is only renewable to the extent you invest in it

I have encountered three types of teams in my career as a social impact communicator:

- **Type 1:** Teams whose leaders acknowledge their superpowers and accelerate them
- **Type 2:** Teams that decide to use their superpowers and unite for good, in spite of an unsupportive leader
- **Type 3:** Teams that crumple because of a lack of cohesion and an unsupportive leader

This points out a fundamental principle that can transform our social impact work if we acknowledge it: teamwork is only renewable to the extent you invest in it. Types 1 and 2 invest in themselves, whether thanks to a leader or in spite of one. Type 3 illustrates the greatest risk, which is having a team unable to support itself and unable to find a leader who will make it great.

The teams whose leaders champion them and encourage them tend to grow strong and mighty. The same is true for teams that band together even without a strong leader. In both cases, their influence is far-reaching. Their impact is awe-inspiring. There's nothing they can't do.

Conversely, teams that struggle tend to operate on borrowed time. Eventually, some team members hunker down and become more stoic and reserved while others depart. They figure they could be happier somewhere else where their unique values and talents are appreciated.

The good news is teams can fuel themselves. Leadership is essential. But some of the greatest leaders I've met don't hold executive titles. They're simply so passionate about their social impact work that they stick with it. They encourage their colleagues. They succeed in spite of the headwinds they face.

I hope you are blessed with incredible leadership that acknowledges and emboldens your work performance. I hope your leader recognizes the gem of a person they've got the privilege of working with.

CHAPTER 4   SECRET #4: HIGHLY EFFECTIVE SOCIAL IMPACT COMMUNICATORS ...
             EMBRACE THE RENEWABLE FUEL OF TEAMWORK

You do important work every day advancing a more equitable world. You help the rest of us hear the stories we need to hear. You work well with others. You identify needs and propose solutions. You use your personal values and communications skills to bring us new insights, perspectives, and opportunities to take action. You are pouring into your teammates, and they are pouring into you—time, compassion, ideas, and encouragement.

All of this investment is important because you will invariably face setbacks that threaten to take this renewable fuel and turn it on its head.

In the next chapter, we'll explore how you as a social impact communicator can respond to moments that threaten to set you back. Instead of caving, you can reframe those experiences as the crest of a hill.

Because beyond that hill is the next great chapter of your change-making adventure.

Key Questions

- Reflect on great teams you've been a part of. What did they have in common?

- As a communicator, you are also a leader. How can you do both effectively?

- What risks do great teams take? How do they approach decisions that could be risky? Why do they decide to take calculated risks?

- What are three key benefits of teamwork for social impact communications projects, compared to tackling a project alone?

- What three encouragements do you hope to impart to any team member under your direction, given that you are a highly effective social impact communicator?

CHAPTER 5

Secret #5: Highly effective social impact communicators ... reframe every setback as the crest of a hill

This is the chapter where I'm supposed to tell you everything is going to be OK. And often, your stickiest situations turn out for the best.

But to be an effective social impact communicator—and thus, bring out the best in any circumstance—you must rethink your thinking about setbacks.

I want you to imagine your hardest days not as challenges to overcome but as the crest of a hill you're equipped to successfully climb past.

That's why we're going to spend the next few pages focused on developing a resilient social impact communicator's mindset within you. To do the type of work you do, it's imperative you have access to every fiber of your being. Every shred of resolve.

Those who get beyond get the change they seek.

CHAPTER 5 SECRET #5: HIGHLY EFFECTIVE SOCIAL IMPACT COMMUNICATORS ... REFRAME EVERY SETBACK AS THE CREST OF A HILL

I know you've got what it takes because I've observed hundreds of social impact leaders navigate this complex work and achieve amazing outcomes. I've seen the power of reframing one's mindset as applied to industries as eclectic as agriculture, food, media, and technology.

It begins by coming to terms with the challenges you face. You decide to lock eyes with those challenges, then shift your perspective—as if you were turning the dial at the end of a kaleidoscope. When you change the way you see the same set of facts, you begin to discover the challenges you and your organization face can be solved. They are not impossibly tall cliff faces. They are hill crests with immense possibilities lying just beyond the horizon.

It turns out

- Your problems might be less big than you think
- Your problems might be more approachable than you realize
- Your problems might be more similar to those of 99% of other social impact communicators
- Your problems might be more empowering than isolating
- Your problems might set you in community rather than set you apart

The crest of a hill exists to be hiked past. It hides the dawn just beyond it.

But to get there, you have to climb and keep climbing. There are plenty of hill crests sitting lonely in the distance because no one has bothered to broach them. They seem too big or scary or ominous.

So together, you and I are going to crest your biggest hills—the gnarly challenges and scary situations you face as a social impact communicator—and hike them together.

You don't need to share all the sordid specifics of your personal experience. It's good for you to have a grasp of the facts. I want you to work through those mentally and with trusted colleagues who know your situation far better than me. But for now, it's plenty for you to simply say to yourself, "I face daily challenges, and I'm curious how to solve them more effectively while losing less sleep."

Together, in community, you can crest those hills and see the wonderful opportunities beyond them.

Let's explore a framework for acknowledging and overcoming setbacks to take your social impact communications talent to the next level.

New insights yield new direction—and the potential for disorienting doubt

Social impact work is quite new, as we have discussed. Some organizations have worked on climate change, equity, and other issues for decades. But in the wider professional world, we have a narrower timeframe of deep experience to draw on.

Most of us, if we're being honest, are still figuring it out.

Ordinarily, this is exciting. It's energizing to help solve big challenges. It spurs on that renewable fuel of teamwork, which we unpacked together in Chapter 4.

But these exciting new vistas have a shadowy side that's less comfortable to talk about and easier to ignore.

I'm talking, of course, about doubt. The questions that begin to emerge in your mind as you get deeper into social impact work start out innocently and can quickly escalate into a thunderous roar.

Traditional communications require a lot of elbow grease yet have clearly defined processes, generally. For example, you know how to interview a subject matter expert, or write a news release and send it through your organization's executive review process.

CHAPTER 5 SECRET #5: HIGHLY EFFECTIVE SOCIAL IMPACT COMMUNICATORS ... REFRAME EVERY SETBACK AS THE CREST OF A HILL

Social impact communications require a lot of elbow grease, too—and few analogs to help you navigate how exactly it should be done. For example, you must often draw out signals in mounds of data, commit to a specific communication strategy about topics that can polarize, and measure the impact and outcomes your organization is having in the world.

The former activities feel safe. The latter activities feel a bit more risky. If we're not careful, the exciting glow of social impact work can fade under the sinister shadow of the unknown.

Let's consider how this looks in your world. Imagine you have launched a new public-private partnership program. You have co-created a vision of the types of work you will do, in partnership with other organizations helping you implement social impact work.

You believe in your heart the work is important. You understand the role each partner will play. You talk semi-frequently. (Perhaps you don't enjoy late-night Waffle House dinners weekly, but that level of relationship takes time. Don't beat yourself up!)

Despite everything going for you, those quiet moments in between all the meetings and emails and deliverables lead you to self-reflection.

Too often, this looks like self-sabotage: Are we really headed in the right direction? Our partners are awfully quiet. Are they starting to doubt where we're headed? Have they lost hope? There are so many other things they could be doing. What's keeping them here? Are we doing everything we can to do the most good? What happens if our partners change course? What will be left of our dream? What are all the ways we might disappoint the people we're trying to help?

In my work as a consultant, I've discovered these moments of self-doubt are perfect opportunities to stop and reflect on everything you've learned so far. When you do this, you put fear on the sidelines so you can appreciate reality in context.

That word—context—is key. When you spiral into negative series of questions, you start believing everything you've experienced up to now has been a sham (a.k.a. imposter syndrome).

CHAPTER 5   SECRET #5: HIGHLY EFFECTIVE SOCIAL IMPACT COMMUNICATORS ... REFRAME EVERY SETBACK AS THE CREST OF A HILL

That's simply not true. Your progress is not an illusion. And a setback doesn't erase all the strides you've made.

Instead, start by facing your doubts about the challenges you face and acknowledging them like an unwelcome relative at Thanksgiving. You love them but won't tolerate their rude behavior.

Here's a simple exercise you can do to acknowledge and put to rest unhelpful thinking about challenges:

1. First, get a blank piece of paper and something to write with. Turn the paper on its side in a horizontal position.

2. Second, draw the letter "S" in large font three times across the entire width of the page. Give each "S" enough surrounding whitespace so you can jot down a few words next to it.

3. Third, notice that each "S" curve represents your journey through specific problems you face (or have faced in the past) in your career as a social impact communicator. Each "S" begins at the bottom of the page (the start of a challenge), winds upward (what author Scott Belsky calls the "messy middle"), and ends with a final curve at the top (overcoming your challenge and moving past it).

4. Fourth, label each "S" curve to illustrate to yourself how you've navigated three complex problems in the past. At the bottom of each "S," write the goal you set out to achieve. This could include producing a video series on farmers facing a changing climate, or publishing a white paper, or delivering a series of talking points to a funding partner. Next, label the

middle of each "S" with the challenge you faced en route to fulfilling your vision. It might be a difficult project or an undefined process or an unsupportive partner. Finally, at the top of each "S," write what you and your team did to overcome the challenge and crest that tricky hill. How did it all work out?

When you are finished, it will look something like this:

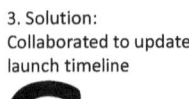

3. Solution: Collaborated to update launch timeline

2. Challenge: Unexpected delays

1. Goal: Produce farmer videos

3. Solution: Identified new experts to contribute insights

2. Challenge: Out-of-pocket subject matter experts

1. Goal: Publish a whitepaper

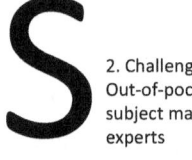

3. Solution: Listened actively and made requested changes

2. Challenge: Funder asks for series of revisions

1. Goal: Deliver talking points to funding partner

Do this just a few times and you'll discover you're much more capable of overcoming challenges than you realize. In a moment, we'll go deeper and think critically about *how* you mustered the internal and external resources to identify hill crests and overcome them. For now, simply acknowledge you are an extremely capable and ingenious social impact communicator ready to solve even the hairiest problems. Give yourself some credit.

I hope this exercise brings a smile to your face. What we're doing is exposing your capacity for good. It's easy to overlook this in favor of everything that's not working. Social impact communicators are among the quickest to become discouraged because amid so many new things, and so many uncertain tracks with no clear road map, discouragement and hopelessness can set in. Just like that Thanksgiving meal that never seems to end.

CHAPTER 5   SECRET #5: HIGHLY EFFECTIVE SOCIAL IMPACT COMMUNICATORS ...
REFRAME EVERY SETBACK AS THE CREST OF A HILL

You hereby have my permission to politely tell these badly behaved holiday guests to take a hike. They've undoubtedly got their own hills to climb. You are empathetic to them and their journey, but they will have to solve their own problems in due time, thank you very much.

Now that you see you are completely capable of working through setbacks, you have what it takes to dig a bit deeper. You now need to reverse engineer the process of reframing setbacks as the crest of a hill.

Let's turn our attention there next.

Crest-climbing insight No. 1: Hills provide unprecedented perspective

My wife and I relocated our family to a small farm in eastern Missouri. If you've ever moved, you know the process can be a big ol' hill. But we had a clear vision of what we were doing and why.

We wanted to get closer to her family in the St. Louis area. We aimed to be nearer to the airport so I could see my family scattered across the western United States. We desired to be closer to our church, in which we are active.

Our property is surrounded by rolling cattle pastures and fields of alfalfa and soybeans. We quickly came to appreciate the perks of being on top of a hill: every sunrise looks like a scene out of an idyllic American painting. Hay bales, tractors, red barns, and fences dot the landscape. We can see for miles.

Being on top of a hill provides perspective. It allows you to look down at where you've been. It lets you scan the horizon to where you're going next.

But to fully appreciate the beauty of the hills that dot the landscape of your social impact work, you must first learn to see them as gifts rather than curses.

CHAPTER 5   SECRET #5: HIGHLY EFFECTIVE SOCIAL IMPACT COMMUNICATORS ...
                REFRAME EVERY SETBACK AS THE CREST OF A HILL

And what curses they can be, at least as we imagine them. In the natural world, you discover it's hard to plant crops on a hill because erosion can pull the soil away. You're more exposed to the elements because you stand out. Hill climbing causes the muscles and mind to ache.

In the working world, the more hills you face, the less traction you seem to make. The more hills that crop up in your relationships with internal colleagues and external partners, the more frustrated and hopeless you can become. Figurative hills pose real challenges that emotionally, physically, and spiritually hamper our ability to do our most important work.

But guess what? You now know that hills, while tricky, can be reframed as opportunities.

You have perspective.

Crest-climbing insight No. 2: Each hill must be tackled differently, though there are patterns

I have good news and bad news.

The good news is the more hills you climb, the better you get at overcoming those challenges. You learn to get creative with your solutions.

The bad news is each hill presents its own unique obstacles and challenges. There's no template or repeat button.

But you start to spot patterns among the hills. You can use this to your advantage.

Consider a common hill: change orders. A seemingly simple client request can turn into a request to redo or substantially change whole pieces of the communications project you've worked so hard on.

I once helped lead a project of this type. We were developing a series of digital sustainability workbooks for farmers. Our team included a mix of storytellers and technical experts both inside and outside the organization.

CHAPTER 5   SECRET #5: HIGHLY EFFECTIVE SOCIAL IMPACT COMMUNICATORS ... REFRAME EVERY SETBACK AS THE CREST OF A HILL

I anticipated regular reviews of the content to ensure accuracy and accessibility. I didn't anticipate how many subject matter experts would engage and offer input in the process. With each new workbook, we got a little wiser—for example, one of my teammates astutely recommended we request a single point of contact to share edits. This immensely streamlined the process, saving time and leading to happiness all around.

The hills you face require a combination of precedent and prediction. Precedent means you can recall examples of how you and your social impact communications team have tackled a particular challenge in the past. You can review what you've learned, then adjust for the specific situation you're facing.

You get to adapt and overcome that hill crest.

Yet you also need to be adept in prediction. Chances are good some aspect of the problem you face will be new and different. You must consider adding some nuance to your approach. Peruse your network for other social impact professionals who might have tackled a similar problem. How did they do it? What people and tools did they need for the job? How long did it take?

You can also channel your inner journalist to make solid predictions. Ask as many questions as you can think of before getting underway with your new assignment. This isn't a stalling tactic. It's an opportunity to be as informed as possible.

Your goal is to understand so deeply the goals, strategy, and proposed course of action that you fully embrace the leadership function of social impact communications. This enables you to see each hill with all its contours and hidden handholds. You begin to see complete paths from the base of the hill to its peak. You remember how you've done it in the past and factor in what's new and different.

In social impact work, I expect you and I will encounter the new, the different, and the original forever and ever. It comes with the territory.

CHAPTER 5   SECRET #5: HIGHLY EFFECTIVE SOCIAL IMPACT COMMUNICATORS ...
            REFRAME EVERY SETBACK AS THE CREST OF A HILL

What won't change is your ability to spot patterns among the communications projects you work on. Even if you are new to your career, role, or industry, you can apply this framework. Within just a few months, you start to spot patterns you can use again and again to solve problems and climb hills.

Be aware of your surroundings and keep good notes. Use a digital tool to make your notes easily searchable. Embrace an open mind. Keep a running list of questions you want to ask. Be persistently curious. Anything is possible when you sincerely want to know more and do your best.

If you need further evidence this approach works, read *Range* by David Epstein. It's got example after example of people through history who dabbled in all sorts of disciplines. They overcame hills, unlocked value, and discovered deeper meaning in their work because they could cross-pollinate ideas among new experiences and unrelated disciplines.

Crest-climbing insight No. 3: Once you've defined what's hard, you can determine what's possible

What are the biggest tasks you must accomplish in your social impact communications work over the next 90 days? Pull out a notebook. Pick a page and divide it into three columns. Then, in the left-hand column, write down those big tasks you'll be working on. We're going to use your list to bust some myths and give you the confidence you deserve that hill climbing is something you can excel at.

As a communications professional, your list might look something like this:

- Meet all of the campaign launch deadlines for our three biggest clients.

CHAPTER 5 SECRET #5: HIGHLY EFFECTIVE SOCIAL IMPACT COMMUNICATORS ... REFRAME EVERY SETBACK AS THE CREST OF A HILL

- Draft the white paper (or hire it out) and get it to the designer.

- Align on strategy for the launch of our big new product/service/grant program.

- Navigate internal communications as we add new team members and external partners for our social impact work.

- Consistently create and publish compelling thought leadership.

Seems a little overwhelming, doesn't it? I bet your list is longer and more complex. Fear not. Now, we're going to fill out those remaining columns and help you find the way forward.

Over the top of the second column, write "Hardest Part." Over the top of the final column on the right-hand side of the page, write "Potential Solutions."

In my hypothetical list, I would start with "Meet all of the campaign launch deadlines." In my experience, the hardest part of any project launch is getting all the minutiae checked off my list while not dropping any of my other recurring work unrelated to the launch. Because as you know, being a social impact communicator is akin to being a circus performer. So in the second column, I might write something like "Take all the project launch action steps without leaving a mess in the rest of my business."

There. That's uncomfortable. But now, I can see it in writing. I know my biggest problem is somehow handling all the tasks on my plate.

Let's move to the third column. How can I balance these project launches while keeping my team moving forward on everything we're doing? One potential solution might be to bring my team together for a 15-minute brainstorm. There, we could decide who's tackling which elements of each project. I might end the meeting by identifying between one and three things we will stop doing to meet our goal.

CHAPTER 5   SECRET #5: HIGHLY EFFECTIVE SOCIAL IMPACT COMMUNICATORS ...
                REFRAME EVERY SETBACK AS THE CREST OF A HILL

I don't mean *imagining* what you might stop and then continuing with those activities. I mean going cold turkey (an American expression if I ever saw one!) and completely ceasing those activities until the launches are finished.

This three-column exercise isn't the end all be all. You might have a different process. But it's a first step in evaluating what's really ahead and potential steps and sacrifices you could make, at least in the short term. Doing so helps you achieve your biggest social impact goals.

If you like, invite a colleague (or several) to work through each of the hills in your organization coming up in the next 90 days.

When you're through evaluating each hill, you'll have the skeleton outline of a strategy for meeting your quarterly goals. You'll walk away more than satisfied that you did your highest and best work—for your clients, your organization, and the rest of us who benefit from what you do.

Crest-climbing insight No. 4: Your flawed fear needs a free ride home

On too many occasions, I've seen a challenge and avoided it. Instead of climbing the crest of the hill, I ran laps around the base.

It's understandable. You face situations with no clear solution all the time, and that feels scary.

There's the potential a campaign won't land the way you expected. A conversation you need to have could upend the stability of your project or team. Your organization's impact might be smaller than expected, or even nonexistent.

Sure, bad things happen. But more often than not, our fears are overblown. They kick in the moment we spot the crest of a hill. They shout through an imaginary megaphone until we give up or timidly approach what we'd normally do with boldness.

Put fear on a nice, air-conditioned bus and send it home. Offer to pick up the tab. Your unfounded fears get in the way of your ability to make breakthroughs and to make a difference. Tone it down to the point you can make rational, calculated decisions. Your team and your audience are counting on you to move forward in spite of fear.

Crest-climbing insight No. 5: You can't climb all the hills today

Here's the rub: every time you reach the summit of a hill, you discover there are more hills beyond. Struggles and obstacles are part of the human condition. They contribute to your daily social impact communication work. They might feel all-consuming.

This can push us to sacrifice our own well-being, family, and personal life. We push forward over the hills in our work because, we reason, there isn't time to stall. Existential dread consumes us. To use an example from my consulting experience, leaders reason that failure to make bold climate action means a broken world for our children and grandchildren. Guess whose fault that will be?

Urgency is important as a tool that spurs us on to do meaningful work. Social impact organizations like yours see positive change not only as possible but as necessarily achievable.

But urgency without attention to your personal well-being is doomed to fail. We need real, authentic, empathetic human beings—you!—to do this work.

I can recall a day I looked at my calendar and discovered I had 11 meetings scheduled back to back. I got through it, all right, but I'm not sure I brought my best self by the time I entered double digits.

In a similar way, see troubling patterns in your own mindset and workflow, and give yourself grace. Take care of your mind, your body, and your family. Get help from trusted peers and leaders to balance your schedule and your projects so you can be *effective*—not just productive.

CHAPTER 5   SECRET #5: HIGHLY EFFECTIVE SOCIAL IMPACT COMMUNICATORS …
            REFRAME EVERY SETBACK AS THE CREST OF A HILL

The hills are far too many to number. Overextending yourself won't change that. Instead, celebrate yourself whenever you climb that hill. See where you've been. Rest up afterward so you can bring your whole self and full passion to the mission tomorrow.

You've got something special. Don't get discouraged. Get convicted: you are making a difference.

Great social impact communicators build a resilient mindset to keep going in the face of adversity

I see you, my readerly friend. That skeptical look on your face. That sinking sense you've heard all this nonsense before. I won't fault you if you've got a raised eyebrow. I am, after all, speaking only from my personal experience. It's easy for me to sit back in my farm office, roosters (or children) crowing in the background, and tell you how to evaporate all your problems.

Don't take my word for it. I saw your resistance from a mile away—because I too doubt whether I can overcome big challenges. I asked other social impact communicators to share their best advice, just for you. I'll introduce insights they shared with me in just a moment, and in the chapters that round out this book.

Because highly effective social impact communicators care deeply about *how* this work gets done. They're not only concerned about outcomes that change society for good, as important as those are. They want everyone—you, your team and your audience—to be positively changed by the experience of social impact work.

Day after day. Week after week.

If you doubt you've got what it takes, these social impact communicators will reassure you that you can do this.

CHAPTER 5 SECRET #5: HIGHLY EFFECTIVE SOCIAL IMPACT COMMUNICATORS ... REFRAME EVERY SETBACK AS THE CREST OF A HILL

It starts by building a resilient mindset.

Here's what several experts told me about cresting hills successfully, in their own words:

> *Social impact communicators can guard against and overcome setbacks by ensuring that they have a level of transparency that is unparalleled and then by responding to detractors with speed, consideration, and understanding.*
>
> —Kent Harrison, former vice president of marketing and premium programs, Tyson Foods, Inc.

> *Be open, transparent and genuine. In my opinion, if you want to make a huge impact and you want to be trusted ... it's very important to be genuine and transparent.*
>
> —Martín Casanova, chief dream maker, Thx!, and director, Fudi Food

> *Be humble, stay scientific and skeptical about your own approach. Just because you want to do good does not mean you are right with all that you say.*
>
> —Max Gulde, co-founder and CEO, Constellr

It may sound simplistic, but trust and transparency are incredibly useful strategies for overcoming setbacks. If you are open in your communications and act with integrity, others are willing to look past the inevitable missteps that can happen in the pursuit of social impact communications. While trust and transparency are important in any aspect of communications, the emotionally charged nature of social-impact communications make these two aspects even more critical, in my opinion. Beyond that, trying to "fake it" when it comes to social impact

CHAPTER 5   SECRET #5: HIGHLY EFFECTIVE SOCIAL IMPACT COMMUNICATORS ...
REFRAME EVERY SETBACK AS THE CREST OF A HILL

communications is just a bad idea. Own your (inevitable and often painful) mistakes, learn from them and grow. Do the work to be better. I know very few people who won't respect that.

—Deron Johnson, executive vice president, Chief Brand + Culture Officer, Curious Plot

Did you notice some patterns? Let's connect the dots to form what I call the Resilient Mindset Playbook. Consider this the daily workout regimen that gets you over hills you face daily as a social impact communicator.

Act with integrity

In one of my workshops, I coach social impact communicators through the design and implementation of their own social contract. In its simplest form, a social contract as I define it is a written document that clarifies

- Your values
- Your process for putting those values to work with people

There's more to it, of course, but those are the fundamentals. In 1689, John Locke famously introduced the concept of the social contract. In his view, social contracts held society together. They gave us a foundation for agreeing on how we wished to be governed and achieve peace. (I'm grossly oversimplifying; you may freely direct irate letters to my inbox.)

Scholars debate the finer points of how we achieve agreement or consent and whether this is a valid way to do things. That's not what you and I are here to do. We are here to remember the foundation of social impact hill climbing is acting with authenticity and kindness. Showing up and strengthening your relationships with other human beings.

As Curious Plot's Johnson points out, this builds trust. It's something you can't buy with money, time, or sheer force of will.

CHAPTER 5   SECRET #5: HIGHLY EFFECTIVE SOCIAL IMPACT COMMUNICATORS ... REFRAME EVERY SETBACK AS THE CREST OF A HILL

Lead with humility

You aren't going to make the right decision every time. Accept it. Own the mistakes you make. Learn and grow.

Social impact work sounds like fun to many people. And oh what fun it can be! These are exciting times, and we have bigger networks and more tools than ever to do good in the world.

Yet you must balance this exuberance with the stone-cold reality that sometimes, the work just isn't fun. It doesn't go how we expected. We make a misstep. We lose face.

But you know what? You can have as many redos as you like. You can apply the principles we've identified in this book about how highly effective social impact communicators work. These aren't earth-shattering truths. They're things you knew all along and simply didn't have the time or the framework to critically evaluate.

You aren't just an executive or a writer or an editor or a project manager.

You are a leader. So lead.

Show us what it looks like to bounce back and do great work after a failure. Take confidence in the strength of your values and the caliber of your talent and training. Stay humble enough to know that even with everything that's working in your favor, you still trip up now and again.

To err is human, as Alexander Pope wrote. That's OK.

Be scientific in your approach

I love the observation Constellr's Gulde makes about staying scientific amid challenges. A scientific approach is essential for the technical aspects of your team's work. Yet it's also an important approach for implementing repeatable systems and processes so your social impact communications hit their mark.

This means doing your homework. It means making hypotheses. It means performing experiments (yes, even communicators can act as if they were wearing a lab coat). It means learning from observation.

When things go wrong, are you tempted to throw the flasks and microscopes out the window and start from ground zero? I know I am, at times.

You don't need to do that. Allow curves in the road to ignite hope rather than hopelessness. For example, say to yourself, "I wonder what might work instead?"

Avoid the doom loop of desperation. You can't help the people who need the clear and compelling messages you offer when your own self-talk is confused and all over the map.

See the hill. Map the path over the crest. Remind yourself and those around you about where you're going. Paint the picture of what you'll see when you get to the top.

Stay skeptical

In the absence of communication, I get antsy. I could tell you stories about times when a client stopped talking to me. Emails dried up. Instant messages sat unanswered.

My takeaway? The relationship is over. We're toast. And I'm the one to blame.

Wouldn't you know it, hours or days later, the conversation picked up again as if nothing had happened. Because *nothing had happened*. I'd invented a made-up story that turned out not to be true.

The same can happen in reverse. You get so close to your social impact communications that you lose sight of possible gaps or flaws. When someone says, "I don't get it" or "This needs work," you immediately leap to defensiveness. (I hope you don't leap across the table at them, though you might be tempted.) How dare they question your handiwork? This is your artisanal gem!

CHAPTER 5   SECRET #5: HIGHLY EFFECTIVE SOCIAL IMPACT COMMUNICATORS ... REFRAME EVERY SETBACK AS THE CREST OF A HILL

Appreciate your craft while acknowledging you can only get better through continuous improvement. Embrace a baseline level of skepticism. This reinforces humility and leaves you open to asking more questions that help you improve at what you do.

As you get better, you help more people. That's the promise of social impact communications.

Communicate with transparency and openness

In my free email newsletter for social impact communicators (go sign up right now at SilverMapleStrategies.com—it takes two seconds!), I share horrifying and heartwarming experiences from my consulting work. My goals are twofold: accelerate your biggest goals, and equip you with strategies to win the inner game of social impact communications.

Vulnerability is my approach of choice, and so I share things like how one time, I killed an opera star. It's not as bad as it sounds. I blame my youthful haste and lack of fine arts appreciation.

Here's what happened—and how it underscores the value of transparency in your communications.

I had a life-changing internship at the *Detroit Free Press* newspaper, working as an online editor on their website. I made lifelong friendships, fell in love with the Motor City, and came to appreciate the rush and impact of content strategy and creation. But even joy hits a speed bump now and again.

My editor had assigned me to read an Associated Press story about a beloved singer. She asked me to edit it and publish it with a headline of my own making. I focused so intently on the urgency of the assignment, and the pride of earning a senior editor's trust, that I failed to read the story as carefully as I should have. I did what I thought was a bang-up job and hit "Publish."

CHAPTER 5 SECRET #5: HIGHLY EFFECTIVE SOCIAL IMPACT COMMUNICATORS ... REFRAME EVERY SETBACK AS THE CREST OF A HILL

Soon after, my editor gave a shout. She drew my attention to the fatal (ahem) flaw: The opera star hadn't died, as my headline claimed. She faced a serious illness instead.

My editor could have taken me to task, but she didn't at all. Instead, she chose to give me what I needed: clear, unequivocable feedback that my oversight was subpar and not true. I needed to step up and own the discipline of thoroughness and accuracy.

You as a social impact communicator should similarly be transparent and open without trampling all over your values. I've never forgotten that moment on the Freep.com news desk, partly because of the embarrassment but mostly because it's a good reminder to remain disciplined. To commit to accuracy. To communicate clearly and constructively.

At some point, you might encounter detractors to your social impact mission. People might think you mishandled a story. Or that your communications campaign or program isn't helping the environment or building equity, or whatever it is you do.

In these cases, listen and communicate. Maybe you're in the right, or maybe you can elevate your approach. You have heard directly from the experts I've shared with you: Be open about your intentions, and value others' perspectives. Take the initiative to create or refine your organization's plan for managing criticism or concerns about your social impact work.

Don't compromise your values or hide in a corner. Instead, cultivate a culture of openness and transparency that leaves you and everyone on your team feeling whole. One that advances the mission with authenticity and accuracy.

CHAPTER 5   SECRET #5: HIGHLY EFFECTIVE SOCIAL IMPACT COMMUNICATORS ... REFRAME EVERY SETBACK AS THE CREST OF A HILL

After your hike past the crest, learn to navigate the cloud forest beyond

I grew up against the backdrop of the beautiful Rocky Mountains of Colorado. My mom loves hiking, so we frequently spent time circling local lakes and walking through alpine meadows. My parents took us to national parks across the United States. We experienced nature in all conditions, whether in glorious sunshine or gullywasher rainstorms.

Nature and social impact work are a lot alike in the sense that they come at you in one big experience. The ups and downs, the sun and the rain. You don't get to order the weather around. The weather will be whatever's in store that day, thank you very much.

This can be disorienting. In some parts of the world, such as tropical areas, cloud forests emerge. There, clouds hang low, touching treetops and reaching below the canopy. Out in the Midwest where I live, I can go outside on certain mornings and see fog draped along the hills like holiday garland. It's strikingly pastoral and also slightly eerie.

If you find yourself with that spooky feeling even after moving past a crest of a hill in your social impact organization, know that it's normal. You've faced your fears, navigated challenges, and thrived to work another day.

Now, you've arrived at the cloud forest. You might be thinking

- When will the other shoe drop?
- What disaster is next?
- If you thought this was hard, just wait—it's going to get worse.
- The stream of chaos is unending. I'll never get a break.
- Where do I go from here?

CHAPTER 5   SECRET #5: HIGHLY EFFECTIVE SOCIAL IMPACT COMMUNICATORS ...
            REFRAME EVERY SETBACK AS THE CREST OF A HILL

Your brain might work differently than mine, but I doubt it. And because I doubt it, I'm pretty sure this type of thinking, while natural—the inner critic is strong!—isn't particularly helpful.

Instead, I want you to stop and find a stone or a fallen log to sit on. There are plenty of them on this imaginary social impact hill hike you and I are taking together.

This act of pausing is actually stone-cold serious. If you ever get lost in the real-life woods, and you don't have a way to navigate your way out, experts advise you wait. Here's how the US Forest Service, which manages government-owned forests in my country, describes it:

> *As soon as you realize you may be lost: stop, stay calm, stay put. Panic is your greatest enemy.*

Now, I'm going to give you some original Nate Birt advice: I want you to take a big sip of WATER. (Yes, you may throw an egg now. Every time an acronym is born, a consultant gets his wings. You may debate where we end up for all of eternity.)

As we close out this chapter together, let's break down this acronym. It's my gift to you, a final tool you can apply to your social impact communications work after you've succeeded in cresting a hill.

<u>W</u>ait

After a struggle, it's natural to start making decisions right away, almost before you have time to process what's just happened.

Stop that. Walk away from your computer. Ask for a break. Hold everything.

Waiting can be doubly important in a high-stakes or emergency situation, so it's important to get into the habit now.

It's so hard to do, and it feels so wrong. But trust me when I stress you need time to reorient.

CHAPTER 5   SECRET #5: HIGHLY EFFECTIVE SOCIAL IMPACT COMMUNICATORS ...
             REFRAME EVERY SETBACK AS THE CREST OF A HILL

You've been through a lot. You've got a long journey to go. (Remember, social impact work is a marathon, and it's especially grueling at this elevation.)

Although we're in the cloud forest, the clouds eventually break apart a bit. You start to see the way forward. At the very least, you begin to determine the next right step to take. And it's easier when you stop to breathe that fresh mountain air.

Analyze

Next, take stock of your surroundings. You've just worked through some challenges and learned some things.

What did you take away, exactly? How will you document your insights? More importantly, how will you apply those insights to avoid or better overcome such challenges in the future?

Debrief with yourself. Your organization probably conducts such after-action reviews regularly. But we rarely take a moment to engage in conversation with ourselves. (I credit my business coach, Ed Gandia, with introducing me to the higher self—the better, wiser, more mature you who is always ready to share perspective and encouragement.)

Use this internal reflection to rediscover hope, remember who you are, and recall why you're doing this work.

Take Gratitude

You've got a lot going for you, my friend. I mean, a lot.

You can't see this fact easily because you're in the thick of things. You're tromping across the landscape. You're planting trees and restoring wildlife habitat. You're cresting the hills and summoning the internal fortitude to tackle three more challenges up ahead.

CHAPTER 5   SECRET #5: HIGHLY EFFECTIVE SOCIAL IMPACT COMMUNICATORS ...
            REFRAME EVERY SETBACK AS THE CREST OF A HILL

Stop right there. I demand you take a WATER break. It's vital to acknowledge where you've come from and how you've grown. Remember all the glorious valleys and sweeping sunsets you've been privileged to witness.

Not every day is a hill. In fact, hopefully many are not. Be thankful and grateful for that.

Evaluate Options

Now that you've basked in the glow of all those fond social impact communications memories, it's time to map your next move.

What will get you one step closer to your social impact communications goals? What will give you the greatest peace of mind as your head hits the pillow tonight? What would uplift your team and external partners faster than just about anything else?

Do that thing. And then, consider the next thing.

The downhill stretch on the other side of the hill crest might feel scary at first. But your pace picks up, and you'll be down the hill and off to the next adventure in no time.

Run Again

By Jove, you did it! You overcame the hill and survived! Now, you get to run.

Look for opportunities to return to your flow state. Celebrate the experience. Trade your hiking boots for running sneakers. Then, take off.

You might experience feeling a little freer and a little lighter. Enjoy it.

You've grown and learned more about what it takes to successfully navigate the emergent landscape of social impact communications.

CHAPTER 5   SECRET #5: HIGHLY EFFECTIVE SOCIAL IMPACT COMMUNICATORS ... REFRAME EVERY SETBACK AS THE CREST OF A HILL

The watchout and the opportunity

I don't want to delay your journey because now you're going places. When you learn to reframe any challenge you face as the crest of a hill, anything is possible.

But I do want to leave you with one watchout and one opportunity.

The watchout is this:

Don't go looking back at and revisiting past events to an unhealthy degree. Once a hill is behind you, do what you can to walk away.

It's one thing to acknowledge and own mistakes and errors in judgment. It's one thing to resolve to do better. It's another to rehash and relive the past in a way that puts you no closer to the finish line—and in fact makes you more vulnerable to overwhelm, sorrow, and regret.

Always look ahead more than you look behind.

Now for the opportunity. As you get better and better at reframing, you can and should become a mentor to others so they can do the same. Start with the team that helps you do the social impact work you love. Help them reframe setbacks and navigate through them. Look for ways to encourage them.

As your team gets better and better, you can equip your partners or clients for hill climbing, too. It's tremendously rewarding to give others the self-confidence, optimism, and strategies for successfully traversing the inevitable hills of social impact work. Bonus: It also boosts your collective work and impact because you increasingly operate from the same playbook.

You're now ready for the next chapter where we acknowledge that, big hurdles aside, things will still be messy. In fact, in social impact work, things have always been messy.

CHAPTER 5   SECRET #5: HIGHLY EFFECTIVE SOCIAL IMPACT COMMUNICATORS ...
            REFRAME EVERY SETBACK AS THE CREST OF A HILL

Hikes through nature have bugs and mud and oppressive heat. Social impact work has ... well, you'll see in a moment.

Grab your hiking stick and some mosquito netting. We're about to get messy.

Key Questions

- Name three setbacks that threatened to derail your social impact communication work. How did you work around them?

- Who specifically helped you navigate setbacks? What did they say or do that made such a difference?

- What will you do first the next time you encounter an obstacle?

- How quickly are you able to see a potential setback on the horizon? How do you get better at spotting and overcoming these? How might you better warn others so they can apply the lessons you've learned?

- What's the first step you will take after successfully overcoming your next setback?

CHAPTER 6

Secret #6: Highly effective social impact communicators ... cede perfection to the messy reality of change-making

Life on a farm is messy. You would think from all the videos available online that farming is pastoral, peaceful, and calm generating. Maybe that's true sometimes. But in general, it's a combination of hard work, trial and error, and uncertainty.

On my family's small farm in Missouri, we raise chickens for eggs, meat, and shows throughout the year. Come fair time, my wife, Julie, and our children get these beautiful birds dressed up to the nines. Yes, even chickens need a bath.

That's the fun part.

CHAPTER 6   SECRET #6: HIGHLY EFFECTIVE SOCIAL IMPACT COMMUNICATORS … CEDE PERFECTION TO THE MESSY REALITY OF CHANGE-MAKING

The messy part includes finding creative ways to fend off all the creatures that love to eat chickens: opossums, raccoons, and skunks among them. It includes ensuring all the feed bins have lids so we don't open a buffet restaurant for the mice. It means checking on chicken pens multiple times each day to ensure they have plenty of food, water, and freedom to graze.

I bet your daily routine as a social impact communicator has some messy parts in it, too. Remember, a social impact communicator is a professional whose job is to use words to open people's hearts. Getting to the root of a question, or solving a complex problem, or even doing something mundane like writing a progress report—all of these things have few straight lines and many unexpected twists.

In this chapter, I want to show you some strategies for getting through the most challenging parts of any social impact mission, program, or project. Even when things are most challenging, a social impact mission is worth sticking with.

One of my favorite books on this topic is *The Messy Middle*, by Scott Belsky. There's a reason Belsky's raw authenticity about his time building amazing software at Adobe is so refreshing. It talks about all the ups and downs of entrepreneurship—the stuff we often forget about (or choose to forcibly blot out of our minds).

Most of us get excited as a new project begins. And who isn't thrilled to close the chapter on a big program into which we've poured every fiber of our being?

But the middle? Well, yuck. At least sometimes.

Let's figure out some ways to make the middle, with all its mess, fun again. Here we go.

CHAPTER 6   SECRET #6: HIGHLY EFFECTIVE SOCIAL IMPACT COMMUNICATORS ... CEDE PERFECTION TO THE MESSY REALITY OF CHANGE-MAKING

How messy looks for social impact communicators

Let's define "messy" super simply for the sake of our coffee chat here. (You do have caffeine, don't you?) Here it goes: messy means the complex relationships, questions, and situations that naturally arise when you work with other human beings in your business.

These are all the things you encounter daily in your social impact work with no clear-cut answer.

I first encountered this type of messy situation completing progress reports. Although funders often have a template for these types of updates, the process of gathering your thoughts, deciding which details to highlight, and acknowledging all of the things you don't yet know can be messy. Filling out a progress report is a necessary routine that often leaves me feeling as if I'm grasping at straws, no matter how many times I've done it.

Consequently, my inner critic loves to get active at moments like this. He asks me a thousand questions, including the following:

- What else can I say about this project we've led for months?

- What would our funding partner most care to know?

- How can I be truthful about how far we've come, and where we're going, without glossing over the fact that we're still learning and adapting?

What I've discovered is that progress reports are a proxy for any social impact communication activity that requires you to tame your messy mindset. You don't have to be Shakespeare, but you do need to appreciate the value of telling a compelling story. A clear story puts structure and meaning to all of the details you *could* share and brings forward the insights you *must* share.

CHAPTER 6   SECRET #6: HIGHLY EFFECTIVE SOCIAL IMPACT COMMUNICATORS … CEDE PERFECTION TO THE MESSY REALITY OF CHANGE-MAKING

The stories that are most engaging to me have a beginning, middle, and end. Consequently, I start with the basics—the beginning, when I complete a progress report. I make sure to

- Remind the reader about the program or project I'm leading.

- State a few of the underlying facts about the program. These details are designed to give the reader an "Aha!" moment so we're quickly on the same page about where we've been and where we're going.

- Comment briefly on the vision we're working to turn into reality.

The middle of the story comes next. Continuing with our progress report illustration, I include details that

- Share what my team has been hard at work on during the reporting period

- Provide data points and anecdotes that illustrate the progress we've made

- Highlight things we've learned or are thinking about doing to be most effective

Finally, I conclude the progress report. (My messy mindset is looking a little less unkempt, at least for this reporting cycle!) I focus on providing some forward-looking remarks. I might

- Indicate what activities my team will undertake next

- Point out what the key outcomes will look like when we complete the project

- Identify any modifications needed for success or describe hurdles we must overcome

None of this is particularly difficult. Yet it does require a sense of wonder and story. A progress report isn't going to become the next blockbuster at your local movie theater. It won't win you any awards. But it will give your funding partner confidence about where you've been and where you're going. In the world of social impact, that means a lot. It means you've successfully navigated your messy mindset and done something worthwhile.

The sticky parts in the middle of a social impact journey are designed to test and mold you personally. They show others you've got what it takes to complete the mission successfully. That's true even though there's no recipe for what you're doing. The middle also gives you and the people around you confidence that you can achieve your goals if you continue chipping away at the opportunity.

Welcome to the messy reality of change-making.

Paint the vision, not Van Gogh

The mess in the middle of your social impact communications efforts has no one-size-fits-all solution. Let me give you a (non-social impact) example. When my family and I recently cleaned out my late grandparents' Tennessee farmhouse, we didn't go in with a carefully orchestrated blueprint about how it would all happen. We hadn't been inside their home in years. We knew we'd probably encounter piles of papers. Drawers and closets packed with clothing and mementos. Perhaps even some animal damage. (Because when you live in the country, critters invite themselves over.)

Rather than spending weeks mapping out a detailed plan, we engaged in conversation with one another. We talked about top priorities—preserving family heirlooms, cleaning out clutter and things we didn't need anymore, pulling out photos and things other family members would want to take home.

CHAPTER 6 SECRET #6: HIGHLY EFFECTIVE SOCIAL IMPACT COMMUNICATORS … CEDE PERFECTION TO THE MESSY REALITY OF CHANGE-MAKING

Try as you might to plan everything to the letter in your social impact work, you're often working at first in broad brush strokes. If you are moving a climate-change program forward, for example, you see the vision and you identify the partners—internally and externally—who will help you.

But you might not fully appreciate what the day-to-day will be like. How many meetings or email conversations will be necessary? Which parts will be hardest, and which will be a piece of cake? How many times will you have to refine your approach before you get the traction you're seeking?

The answers to these questions and others like them will appear only as you do the work. You set goals, of course, individually and as an organization. You are expected to deliver results and progress against the mission and a set of goals.

As the famous psychologist Carl Jung once said:

> *Your vision will become clear only when you can look into your own heart. Who looks outside, dreams; who looks inside, awakes.*

The process of navigating messy circumstances begins with the type of mindset you and I have uncovered throughout this book. It begins with introspection and with an understanding of who you are. You are capable of casting a vision of where you are going so that your team desires to follow.

Early in the part of my career where I focused on climate change, I felt like a fraud. Here I was, surrounded by people with PhDs and advanced theories of change. I simply wanted to help the farmers and ranchers I'd come to love. By pairing up with other compassionate experts, we made—and continue to make—a difference. You do, too.

We aren't Van Gogh. We might not think the canvas on which we're working is particularly stunning. But we share a vision that helps us weather challenges, setbacks, and unexpected delays in our work.

Each day, we can work to reveal a bit more of the vision and its potential.

CHAPTER 6   SECRET #6: HIGHLY EFFECTIVE SOCIAL IMPACT COMMUNICATORS …
CEDE PERFECTION TO THE MESSY REALITY OF CHANGE-MAKING

Why you should embrace satisfied persistence rather than perfection

You aren't a half-doer, are you? You don't start writing a piece of copy and then abruptly walk away when you're 50% of the way there. You don't string meaningless words together in headlines and hope the reader catches the meaning. You don't produce video series free from narration and purpose. You have a strategy, and your social impact communications emerge from that clear direction.

As communicators, our skill isn't just mental toughness. It's also technical skill. None of us wants to send something into the world—especially of this magnitude—without really thinking it through.

Many of my clients employ an accuracy check policy as insurance against error—and the damage it can cause. Once a piece of copy is written, I send it over to the sources I've interviewed with a request to look things over. I want to make sure what I've said is factual. I want to verify I've presented those facts in context. This process has saved me countless embarrassing moments. I've discovered people want to be pleasantly surprised when they see their name in print, or on a video, not startled.

Of course, this is not standard practice in all forms of communication, such as journalism, and that's OK. I use the accuracy check to illustrate the importance of satisfied persistence in a world where, mentally, we'd love for everything to be exactly right the first time. We love to ship things and be done with them.

The truth is—and you might want to sit down for this—you and I don't have it all figured out. Despite our best efforts, as hard as we work, we're going to make mistakes. We get things wrong. We need forgiveness. We can (and must) request do-overs.

Satisfied persistence means accepting your journey as a social impact communicator with all its flaws and wrinkles. Rather than getting discouraged, you keep going. You find solace knowing you and your team are doing your best.

CHAPTER 6   SECRET #6: HIGHLY EFFECTIVE SOCIAL IMPACT COMMUNICATORS …
CEDE PERFECTION TO THE MESSY REALITY OF CHANGE-MAKING

Live events such as conferences and webinars made me aware of the importance of satisfied persistence. Invariably, the technology on stage isn't working exactly like it should. Or a speaker's flight gets delayed, and they must cancel at the last minute. Or a panel discussion you just knew would be riveting for your audience—perhaps it's even about the value of progress reports, a particularly thrilling topic!—falls flat.

In those moments, it's important to remember you've still produced a quality event for other social impact professionals, even if it didn't go exactly to the blueprint. You keep going, striving for better and better outcomes. You also know potholes come with progress.

What I've observed is that no organization, regardless of its social impact successes on behalf of society, has everything figured out. In fact, if anyone claims to have it all figured out, be suspicious. Having a fully baked plan sounds nice—until it breaks in the face of reality. Your business or nonprofit isn't alone in encountering an occasional mess. Satisfied persistence is a mindset tool designed to remind you that social impact efforts are worth the investment you make.

Name another job you'd rather be doing—another cause you'd rather advance.

Let me shift from the preachy to the practical. You can sit with the concept of abandoning perfection, sure. But what steps and actions should you take to do so?

Allow me to explain in the next section. As you read, consider which insights might be most relevant for you and your team—and which might need modification to fit your specific situation.

No single approach cuts through all the mess. Follow the principles we've discussed elsewhere in this book, and you will make progress no matter what. If you find progress is impossible, perhaps it's time to consider a change in your organization or your career that enables you to practice, without reservation, the secrets of highly effective social impact communicators.

CHAPTER 6   SECRET #6: HIGHLY EFFECTIVE SOCIAL IMPACT COMMUNICATORS ... CEDE PERFECTION TO THE MESSY REALITY OF CHANGE-MAKING

Stop trying to tie up all the loose ends

One of the most effective procrastination methods at the disposal of a social impact communicator is to keep refining something to death. Rather than launching the campaign or publishing the whitepaper, you decide it needs one more round of review. You need to find a couple more supporting illustrations or data points. We need to time it just right for maximum impact.

All those things might be necessary. On the other hand, there could be something else holding us back. Maybe you want things to be perfect when, in reality, satisfied persistence would tide you over—and get your important insights out into the world.

The topic of bringing things to an end the right way has been well documented. As the book *Necessary Endings* by Dr. Henry Cloud notes:

> *Endings are a natural part of the universe, and your life and business must face them, stagnate, or die. They are an inherent reality.*

Fantasy looks like trying to tie up all the loose ends before we take a leap of faith. Reality is moving forward with imperfect circumstances and knowledge, trusting you'll get your point across in the most professional way possible. There are no guarantees in social impact communication, but neither are there excuses for extreme delay. To reap the benefits of your products, services, and programs, and to avoid the risks of a world without them, you must eventually put down loose ends and move ahead.

This requires discretion. You must not compromise on your organization's review policy for content, for example. There can often be compelling reasons for crossing Ts and dotting Is many times over. Know where those guardrails lie, honor them, and then ship the campaign, launch the service, announce the program.

We all benefit when you take action.

CHAPTER 6   SECRET #6: HIGHLY EFFECTIVE SOCIAL IMPACT COMMUNICATORS ...
            CEDE PERFECTION TO THE MESSY REALITY OF CHANGE-MAKING

Move ahead instead of around in circles

A close cousin to tying up loose ends is moving around in circles. You might have heard this called "sideways motion." These are actions that feel good at the time. You are doing stuff! Big or little, the action doesn't matter. What matters is the feeling of task completion.

But as with any activity in your social impact portfolio, you should always ask: Is this action the right action? Is it getting me the results our organization needs?

Going around in circles is akin to a hamster on a wheel. It provides a good mental and physical workout, but you're stuck in place.

One of my clients wanted to track metrics on some of the content it published. I provided friendly reminders to encourage tracking of those data points at regular intervals versus waiting until an urgent progress report required them. Every time I gave such a nudge, guilt nearly ate me up. From my perspective, the division appointed with keeping up the data wanted to be helpful yet didn't have the resources and tools it needed.

Going around in circles when the going gets messy is extremely common across every organization and industry I've observed. It's often because of one or more internal mismatches. You can learn to identify (and navigate around) these mismatches. Here are some examples:

- **Bandwidth mismatch:** If you keep having the same conversation with the same results, a bandwidth mismatch is possible. It might mean your colleagues don't have time in their schedules to complete the task. Other projects have taken precedence. Teams are focused elsewhere because of leaders' guidance, pressing projects, perceived priorities of the organization, or all of the above.

- **How to move ahead:** If you have the authority to push pause on other activities to move your social impact work forward, do so. If it's outside of your hands, go to team members and/or leaders whose help you need and see if you can reach an agreement to get the task done without breaking them or the organization. Keep an open mind and be flexible. Perhaps your project can wait, or maybe they can rearrange their schedules to meet the need you've identified.

- **Urgency mismatch:** You might see something as a pressing concern. Your peers might not see the big rush. You now have some sorting out to do. Get clear on deadlines you need to reach, and to what end. Do you need to submit a proposal before the grant opportunity closes? Are you trying to make a major announcement at a big social impact conference or industry event? Provide your team with all the information they need to see the social impact problem from your vantage point.

  - **How to move ahead:** Have an authentic conversation and explain what you need by when—and why. Offer to help in any way or to provide the necessary people and resources to get the job done.

- **Matrix mismatch:** If you work in a mid- to large-sized organization, you understand the complex yet essential art of managing across different divisions, leaders, and functions. Circular motion can result when multiple divisions need to work together to accomplish a task—yet don't know why or how to do so.

- **How to move ahead:** Assemble your team on a quick call to explain the need. Or go a rung higher on the corporate ladder to find someone with the authority (see "Authority mismatch" below) or the relative independence and decision-making ability to delegate instructions to everyone involved. This can help keep everyone on the same page.

- **Authority mismatch:** If you've ever caught yourself complaining about divisions of your organization feeling walled off from one another, you're normal. But those walls can serve an important purpose. They help us form a community. They enable us to make clearer distinctions between who does which tasks. They permit us to grow and to move up the career ladder in a defined progression. The downside is that when authority is unclear, unexpected confusion can arise. For example, Division A's leader assigns a project to Division B's team member. Unless some clear conversations happen, Division B's team member might face confusion. Is this project merely a favor for a division outside of my wheelhouse? Is it a mandate from the CEO or vice president or another executive that crosses all divisional lines? Should I listen to my own supervisor or this new authority figure? The resulting uncertainty can send you around in circles.

    - **How to move ahead:** Have a clear protocol in place to help you and your team quickly get clarity on whose authority guides your decisions. If your organization is pretty flat and it's an all-hands-on-deck environment, the answer might be, "If anyone says they need help, help them." In other cases where an organization has a more defined leadership structure, you might simply say, "Come talk to me first" or "Ask the president of our division for clarification on what you should be doing." A simple set of standard operating procedures can help you avoid an authority mismatch.

- **Scheduling mismatch:** Do you ever come to the end of the day and wonder why you weren't able to get everything done on your to-do list? Me too. This can create a scheduling mismatch. Maybe you told a colleague you'd get around to completing a task to move your social impact program forward. You simply got tied up with other things. Or maybe you asked a teammate for help and they said, "Come back to me in a week when this assignment is wrapped up." Either way, delays can be frustrating and costly. It isn't personal. It's simply the reality of working in a time-constrained world.

  - **How to move ahead:** See if you can find other people within your organization with comparable skill sets and authority to help you do the task you're needing—pulling the data, analyzing the insights, producing the report. Alternatively, ask yourself: Is this assignment really as urgent as I think it is? Would a week's delay (or whatever other timeframe your colleague needs) hurt our progress? If the answer is "no," it might be best to wait. I bet there are other projects you could work on. If the answer is "Yes, it's now or never," get with your team and think through creative solutions for overcoming the scheduling hurdle. Maybe

**CHAPTER 6   SECRET #6: HIGHLY EFFECTIVE SOCIAL IMPACT COMMUNICATORS …
CEDE PERFECTION TO THE MESSY REALITY OF CHANGE-MAKING**

you need to hire a contractor. Or pause another assignment. Or ask a client for an extension. Overcome scheduling issues to break out of circular motion.

- **Capability mismatch:** Consider whether the people you're asking to do a task are the right people. Are they qualified, based on technical skills and experience, to help? Do they have a proven track record of delivering this kind of information? Wishful thinking won't get you what you need. Take an honest look. Similarly, look at your own skills and shortcomings. Know what you're able to help with and also what you aren't qualified to support in your social impact programming. Be accountable and honest with your leadership team. Shore up areas of weakness or agree that there are certain tasks you won't prioritize—and know who you can call on instead when needs arise.

  - **How to move ahead:** Know thyself, know thy team, and be intentional. Match social impact communications tasks with the right people.

- **Social impact valuation mismatch:** A values mismatch happens when people in your organization value social impact activities differently. You see the grand vision of how your team's work makes the world a better place. Your colleagues see a lot of work with little or no immediate payoff, and plenty of messiness and frustration along the way. Empathy is essential in these cases. Not everyone sees the world the way you do. That's a benefit, not a disadvantage. Diverse perspectives yield better outcomes. The clients and audiences you serve are similarly nuanced. Their brains operate on a spectrum of values, beliefs, and priorities.

- **How to move ahead:** Have a friendly conversation with your skeptical colleague. Point out the opportunities and "so what" of the social impact work you're doing. Invite your division leader or another executive to share the organization's perspective. How does this activity align with the overall mission and vision of the organization? If such discussions don't break through, you might consider delegating the task to someone who understands the social impact mission and is ready to chip in. Stay flexible. You might find it frustrating to not see eye to eye with a colleague. But it's not the end of the road.

As you can probably tell by now, circular motion happens regularly in our organizations. It might feel like the final blow to your hard-earned social impact dreams. But rest assured, it's perfectly normal and overcomeable.

Get creative. Ask for help. Imagine solutions. Pick one and move forward. Experiment. Adjust as needed.

The hamster that gets off the wheel gets the carrot.

When the dust flies, remember it will settle

In the middle of our biggest and most consequential social impact projects, there's going to be dust.

Have you seen pictures of the Dust Bowl that happened in the United States during the 1930s? A combination of land-management practices and environmental conditions converged. Storms carried soil away from

CHAPTER 6 SECRET #6: HIGHLY EFFECTIVE SOCIAL IMPACT COMMUNICATORS ... CEDE PERFECTION TO THE MESSY REALITY OF CHANGE-MAKING

farmers' fields and into the air. The consequences of such dust storms were profound. They removed valuable topsoil essential to growing food and feed crops. They created health hazards, pushing people indoors, pelting their skin, threatening their breathing, and blocking the sun's rays.

Among social impact communicators, flying dust stirred up in the middle of a project can create all kinds of issues. For example:

- A critical deliverable arrives late and underbaked, leading to harsh words, hurt feelings, and a bewildered client.

- A team that seemed glued together comes apart as divisions arise over the strategy best suited to reach the desired outcome.

- A partner organization undergoes a leadership change—and the new leader questions whether your social impact program is worth pursuing further.

- A competitor announces an attractive and well-funded program similar to the one you were about to launch.

- A colleague avoids or glosses over an important discussion that will determine where you go from here.

These types of dust storms aren't more common in malicious cultures or hyper-friendly ones, as far as I can tell. They simply *are*. If you're a human being, you're bound to encounter some type of conflict as you do this work.

You can limit dustups in the first place and settle them faster when they happen by building relationships with your coworkers and by exercising patience.

In the last chapter, I introduced you to several social impact communications experts. They've seen some dust! I wondered: How do they navigate the messy mid-section of social impact projects? Here's what they shared:

CHAPTER 6 SECRET #6: HIGHLY EFFECTIVE SOCIAL IMPACT COMMUNICATORS ... CEDE PERFECTION TO THE MESSY REALITY OF CHANGE-MAKING

In my work leading DEI communications at Curious Plot, one of my go-to pieces of advice to others on our team is to assume positive intent when it comes to evaluating words and actions of others. If someone uses a term in the wrong way, assume they were trying to do the right thing. If someone makes an offensive reference to another person or group, assume they were trying to be respectful. Hand-in-glove with assuming positive intent is to give grace to others navigating the minefields of social-impact communications. Because you know what? One day you'll be the one in need of receiving grace. It's a guarantee.

—Deron Johnson

Know your subject matter better than anyone else and become the absolute expert in the field. Have sincere belief and passion for your ideas and projects and take every public and private opportunity to express that passion.

—Kent Harrison

Keep things simple and explain as detailed as possible the brand purpose or impact. Social impact, ESG and sustainability are trending topics nowadays, however, it's a new field for most people. Teaching it's very important.

—Martin Casanova

Be honest: (1) Acknowledge that your solution is part of a larger puzzle, not the entire solution. (2) Admit that you need most likely help in creating the impact and look for partners. (3) Don't try to make the created impact count as yours alone.

—Max Gulde

In short: Be kind. Be clear. Be a teacher. Be vulnerable. The amount of dust in any social impact project is proportional to the degree to which you work to control it before the project even begins—and right in the heart of it.

CHAPTER 6 SECRET #6: HIGHLY EFFECTIVE SOCIAL IMPACT COMMUNICATORS ... CEDE PERFECTION TO THE MESSY REALITY OF CHANGE-MAKING

Capture attention and direct focus rather than sowing chaos

In his incredible and hilarious book on marketing, titled *Get Different*, author Mike Michalowicz has this to say about the significance of attention:

> *If you offer something that serves, you must make everyone aware. We need you, but we don't know you exist. And that "not knowing you exist" part is your responsibility to fix. Starting immediately.*

As social impact communicators, there are times when we must shift the attention away from someone's negativity or their sideways energy. Capturing attention puts all eyes back on the mission and the tasks you must complete to see it through. As quickly and as orderly as possible.

Once, my parents and I visited a Sunday morning church service as we traveled through Tennessee, where my mom grew up. The worship service began as we expected. But 20 minutes later, when the preacher got up and started delivering his message, the fire alarms sounded. Flashing lights and a blaring klaxon alerted us that something was the matter. The preacher instructed everyone to get up and head toward the doors.

As we approached the hallway, a man motioned for us to stay seated. It turned out this was a false alarm. We seated ourselves once more, the preacher made a few jokes about the unusual circumstances, and he continued the sermon.

Two minutes later, the saga continued. Another person took the stage and whispered something in the preacher's ear.

"It appears we might have a real situation," the preacher said. "Don't stampede, but please proceed to the exits."

CHAPTER 6 SECRET #6: HIGHLY EFFECTIVE SOCIAL IMPACT COMMUNICATORS ... CEDE PERFECTION TO THE MESSY REALITY OF CHANGE-MAKING

This man knew the value of capturing attention and directing focus! He didn't fan people's fears by screaming, "We're all going to die!" or show any outward signs of panic, even though I'm sure he felt concern. He did what the moment required. He directed people where to go so they could stay safe.

(I'd tell you the end of the story, but I'm not sure what happened next. My parents and I were on a trip back home and had hours left to drive. We decided to forego Sermon Part 3. You may now judge me.)

Chaos sometimes feels like a daily occurrence for social impact communicators. Projects grind to a halt. For-sure sales fall through. Marketing campaigns stumble out of the starting gates.

When you face a messy situation, remember the mission. Revisit the earlier chapters of this book. Remember your personal values and the values of your organization. Why are you doing all of this, anyway? These moments help you stay calm so you can pass that calm along to others in your organization.

Here's a framework that might help you decide how to proceed—and bring others alongside you—if a messy situation threatens your plans:

- **Decide what you can do today:** You might need to shift or amend a goal. You might need to build a new project management calendar to accommodate factors outside your control. You might need to simply listen to a teammate. Figure out what you can do today, and do that.

- **Engage your team in dialogue:** Some cases call for discretion and limited sharing because of sensitive information and circumstances. I get that. But whenever possible, use the messy process of change-making to stay glued to your team. Share what's working and what's changing. Ask for feedback. Encourage questions and conversation. You get the privilege of working with some amazing and talented people. Capture their attention with your words and your positive attitude. Direct their focus with your words, and encourage them. Build trust and common understanding. Don't give chaos a seat at the table.

- **Spot chaotic comments and address them directly:** Some people seem thrive on chaos. They make comments packed with TNT. They flit from one team member to another, or one division to another, speculating and wringing their hands. Sometimes, there's malicious intent. Generally, though, this kind of negativity stems from something more sincere such as fear, worry, or uncertainty. If you spot someone fueling a messy situation, find time to speak with them one on one. Explain what you're seeing and how it could be perceived by others. Encourage them to consider alternative words and actions that stick to the facts and empower others rather than unnerving them. Make sure your colleagues feel empowered to approach you directly if you try to plant the seeds of chaos.

You as a social impact communicator are talented in your use of language that opens people's hearts. Use this skill in your technical role and also in your leadership. The resulting calm provides people around you with the psychological safety and space to show up in a way that advances the important work you're doing.

Turn panic into peaceful action

When things get messy, it's difficult to remain calm. Anxiety creeps in and ramps up. We lose track of what we were doing or what step to take next. Our brains and bodies are wired this way. As researchers Catherine A. Hartley and Elizabeth A. Phelps noted in an analysis of stress and anxiety:

CHAPTER 6   SECRET #6: HIGHLY EFFECTIVE SOCIAL IMPACT COMMUNICATORS … CEDE PERFECTION TO THE MESSY REALITY OF CHANGE-MAKING

The amygdala is a key component of the brain systems mediating fear and anxiety and their cognitive effects. At the same time, the prefrontal cortex is critically involved in the control of fear and decreased prefrontal engagement is observed in trait and clinical anxiety. We propose that this shared architecture may yield predictable effects of anxiety on decision-making. Specifically, anxiety increases the attention to negative choice options, the likelihood that ambiguous options will be interpreted negatively, and the tendency to avoid potential negative outcomes, even at the cost of missing potential gains.[1]

Not only are you fighting biology in your role as a social impact communicator but also the rapidly snowballing information you feel compelled to assess.

Our information paralysis is so acute that two-thirds (64%) of us say we'd just as soon have a robot sort through data for us. The figure rises to 70% for business leaders, according to a study from the tech company Oracle.[2]

Overwhelm, it seems, is what we do best these days.

I could stop here and simply observe things are hopeless. But I don't believe that's the case. After all: Your organization gets the benefit of working with *you*.

And because *you* have done the homework, you know that social impact communications are a combination of technical skill and leadership. When you see panic, you raise the stakes with peaceful action. You don't need a PhD in mindfulness or crisis management to know that a kind word, clear directions, and reinforcement of the mission can go a long way.

---

[1] "Anxiety and Decision-Making." Hartley, Catherine A., and Phelps, Elizabeth A. Biological Psychiatry. July 15, 2012. www.ncbi.nlm.nih.gov/pmc/articles/PMC3864559/

[2] "Global Study: 70% of Business Leaders Would Prefer a Robot to Make Their Decisions." Oracle. April 19, 2023. www.prnewswire.com/news-releases/global-study-70-of-business-leaders-would-prefer-a-robot-to-make-their-decisions-301799591.html

CHAPTER 6   SECRET #6: HIGHLY EFFECTIVE SOCIAL IMPACT COMMUNICATORS ...
            CEDE PERFECTION TO THE MESSY REALITY OF CHANGE-MAKING

Do those things. When you start to see the fear in people's eyes, acknowledge it and empathize. Then, communicate how to move forward. Give people confidence and reassurance. And most importantly, try to stay calm.

Guard the silent moments

When the going gets tough, our inner critic and the activity around us rise to a fever pitch. We fill every empty space with action—or thoughts about what action we might take next. We convince ourselves a little more fretting and a little more worry are sure to work out a solution.

They don't. I've tried it often, and it hasn't worked yet.

Instead, what you can do is appreciate those periodic moments when the action stops. When the end of the workday arrives. When you achieve that next milestone.

What happens amid those gaps? Nothing. You should savor that.

In an always-on world where people and brands reach out to our brains via push notifications, social media, or virtual reality, those quiet moments are perfect for reflection. Or simply doing nothing.

Rather than panicking when a silent moment arrives, see it for what it is. Silence during the middle of a major social impact initiative is a gift that allows you to

- Rest your mind
- Restore your hope
- Recharge your creative potential
- Think about something other than the tasks on your to-do lists
- Get creative about where you go next, without the urgency of a pressing deadline

CHAPTER 6   SECRET #6: HIGHLY EFFECTIVE SOCIAL IMPACT COMMUNICATORS ...
CEDE PERFECTION TO THE MESSY REALITY OF CHANGE-MAKING

This appreciation of silent moments doesn't come naturally to me. I bet it won't to you, either. But practice guarding the silent moments anyway. These liminal spaces between major bursts of activity become an oasis in which your mind, body, and soul can find a much-deserved rest.

How can you honor the silence? Here are a few strategies I find useful. See if any of them might work for you:

- **Airplane mode:** When I'm on deadline and not on standby for a major development, I sometimes put my phone on airplane mode. This gives me uninterrupted focus.

- **Calendar yourself:** Schedule meetings with yourself to work on important projects. Give yourself margin. If someone asks you to schedule something in that block, you can honestly say you have a meeting. Keep it, use it, and appreciate the elegance of dedicated "hidden" calendar blocks.

- **Wrap before done:** You are always going to have work to do. Rather than finishing the day when everything is done—a nice thought, but probably not realistic—wrap up *before* you're done. Pick a time on the clock, or a point in the project, and vow to step away. You might need a buddy or a spouse or an energetic child to pry your fingers from the keyboard. You won't regret going cold turkey if you've put in an honest day's work. And I know you do.

- **Structure your days:** Know your preferences and build your workday around them, as much as possible. For example, many people (myself included) prefer mornings for dedicated focus on creative assignments. Afternoons are great for meetings. Rarely can you control every hour, especially in a busy organization. My point is to aim for predictable times on your calendar when you are alone doing focused work, and other times when you are with people in meetings and brainstorming sessions. Predictability helps you develop a cadence and lets you reserve energy proportional to planned activities.

- **Unplug for real:** Raise your hand if you've ever checked work email on vacation. Don't be ashamed. It's happened to many of us. As much as it's within you, though, don't do this. An emergency situation or major initiative might require you to divide free time and work. But try to stick with your schedule. Honor that beautiful time off, including the silent moments. It's hard to restore your remarkable brain, talent, and values if you continue to tax them when you're technically off the clock.

You don't need to be a project management ninja or a life coach to find creative ways to build breaks and rest into your schedule. You simply need to be intentional about it and nominate someone to make sure you invest as heavily in the silent moments as you do everything else. Take care of your future self.

You won't regret it.

CHAPTER 6   SECRET #6: HIGHLY EFFECTIVE SOCIAL IMPACT COMMUNICATORS ... CEDE PERFECTION TO THE MESSY REALITY OF CHANGE-MAKING

Engage in regular conversation that sparks ideas and opportunities

On average, we speak between 15,000 and 17,000 words per day, according to a much-cited study referenced in an article by science magazine *Scientific American*.[3] That means there's ample opportunity to encourage one another through the messy work of social impact.

I didn't always enjoy putting myself out there for the sake of building relationships and having conversations. On the contrary, facing challenges made me retreat into my shell. (I didn't quite go to the extent of living in a pineapple under the sea, or befriending a starfish, but I got awfully close.)

Nudge yourself to engage with your team, your business partners, and your clients. Find opportunities to meet and learn from those you're serving.

You might feel at first as though this is a waste of time. You've got a dozen things to do and not even five minutes to spare—at least, it feels that way. The amazing thing about conversation is that it brings you closer to others. It exposes you to new ideas and experiences that have shaped those around you. In turn, you trade stories.

You discover new information about yourself and the world that could help you make that climate-change program a little stronger. Or lead you to rethink the way you're approaching racial equity in your work. And so on.

You don't need me to tell you how to visit. In some parts of the United States (you know who you are!), it's important to grab a pitcher of sweet tea and find the nearest porch. I'll let you proceed as you see fit. The important thing is to simply go out and do it. Get into the habit. Find excuses to spend time with others, in and out of your organization.

---

[3] "Gender Jabber: Do Women Talk More than Men?" Nikhil Swaminathan. July 6, 2007. Scientific American. www.scientificamerican.com/article/women-talk-more-than-men/

CHAPTER 6   SECRET #6: HIGHLY EFFECTIVE SOCIAL IMPACT COMMUNICATORS … CEDE PERFECTION TO THE MESSY REALITY OF CHANGE-MAKING

Keep a note on your phone or in a journal where you can jot down things you're learning about the people around you and ideas you're encountering. You might be surprised at where your next big breakthrough comes from.

Beyond idea generation, regular conversation amid the messy parts of social impact work has two more benefits that might not be immediately apparent.

First, spending time visiting with others gives you the chance to exercise compassion. The workplace is too often like a marina or an international trade zone. We treat one another like ships passing in the night.

You can counter this trend. Dock your boat and step onto the wharf. Stretch your legs. Apply the leadership discipline of a social impact communicator and show that you care—because you genuinely do.

Your ability to spend time with others illustrates durability. The middle part of any social impact project—a.k.a. the part that actually gets results—is daunting for nearly everyone I know. I bet you love what you do, and I bet you also question what you're doing and why from time to time. This work requires durability. It requires confidence that the investments you and your team make now will pay off later. Show people around you what it means to be durable. You can still be completely vulnerable and raw and real.

Durability is simply resilience with a smile.

Second, regular conversation gives oxygen and time to our relationships. Without convening with other people regularly as we navigate the mess, the ups and downs of purpose-driven work, we rob ourselves of joy and limit the capacity of others to share what's on their hearts and minds.

Have the regular presence of mind to nourish the relationships that make your organization and your mission great. Give generously, asking for nothing in return but a few moments of time. Always add more value to others than you take for yourself.

The results are magical, even though the inputs require no special wizardry.

CHAPTER 6 SECRET #6: HIGHLY EFFECTIVE SOCIAL IMPACT COMMUNICATORS ... CEDE PERFECTION TO THE MESSY REALITY OF CHANGE-MAKING

Trade predictability for adaptability

Let me tie up this chapter by introducing you to my second-oldest son, Titus. I love this young man. From an early age, he has been enamored of time and schedules, and predictability. If mom leaves the room, he needs to know where mom has gone. If we are on vacation, he needs a refresher on the itinerary at least once per hour. If we have had dinner every night at 5:30 for the past five years, he still wants reassurance that dinner is on schedule. (Which it occasionally isn't in a household of six.)

The funny thing is I used to be just like Titus. I probably still am, to some degree, even though I might not say it out loud. Maybe you can relate. We have become so busy, so caught up in the day-to-day intricacies and drama of our social impact work, that predictability becomes our goal. We don't know how we're going to get it all done. We worry whether it's going to be enough, and fast enough. We feel trapped in the middle and grasp for a shovel or a rake or anything to help us break through to the other side.

I'm here to tell you that predictability isn't actually the goal. When you put that high bar to rest, your world will open up and feel far more achievable.

Instead of pursuing predictability, aim for adaptability instead. Recognize that the workplace in general is far too fast-paced and has far too much to accomplish than is realistic to do in a given day. Many social impact initiatives I've led or observed go on for years, sometimes decades. This isn't a fault but rather a function of this type of work.

Rest assured, your communications investments can advance the mission every day, even though the big-picture changes take time.

Cultivate the practice of adapting to your ever-changing circumstances. Adapt your own mindset and approach to the world so that you can ride out each new hill and valley.

See the most challenging days as the crest of a hill (and revisit previous chapters for reassurance). Embrace conversation and time spent with colleagues. Take time to yourself to do the important work that comes with

CHAPTER 6   SECRET #6: HIGHLY EFFECTIVE SOCIAL IMPACT COMMUNICATORS ...
             CEDE PERFECTION TO THE MESSY REALITY OF CHANGE-MAKING

the territory of the middle of any project. Cut yourself off before you get too deep in the weeds and resolve to come back tomorrow, refreshed and ready to tackle the next big opportunity.

As we prepare for our final chapter, this will prove particularly handy. Because your influence—on your organization, your team, and your mission—outlives you.

How do you want to be remembered? The messy nature of change-making won't ever change. But how you show up and how you communicate and lead can change dramatically. It can pave the way for those around you and for future generations.

Let's unwrap the final secret of highly effective social impact communicators by peering into the future of your incredible social impact legacy.

Key Questions

- What three things will you gladly give up or stop doing to avoid the unnecessary heartache/stress/pain they cause at work?

- How can you still do your job without the friction of tying up every loose end?

- What story will you tell yourself the next time something gets messy?

- Who will you consult first when things seem to be falling apart?

- What evidence will you seek that things are more on track than you realize?

CHAPTER 7

Secret #7: Highly effective social impact communicators … build personal and professional legacies that outlive them and their careers

Death forces us to reconsider what we value most in life. It's sneaky like that.

I thought a lot about this as I helped my family clean out my Tennessee grandparents' farmhouse, a process I mentioned earlier in this book. As we sorted through boxes of old newspaper clippings, family photographs, and quilts, it dawned on me that stuff isn't a legacy. Rather, those objects recall a legacy. They bring it to mind once more.

CHAPTER 7   SECRET #7: HIGHLY EFFECTIVE SOCIAL IMPACT COMMUNICATORS ... BUILD PERSONAL AND PROFESSIONAL LEGACIES THAT OUTLIVE THEM AND THEIR CAREERS

Toward the end of our weeklong project tidying up and preserving family heirlooms, I took a walk up the hill and into the field where my grandparents are buried, side by side. They share a headstone that sits away from a group of other, much older graves, where people unrelated to us have been buried for more than a century. The sun shone brightly and the birds sang. I felt sadness at my grandparents' passing. Yet I also felt joy—for the memories I held of them and for the peace that hung in the air around me.

How do you want to be remembered? What do you want your legacy to be? They're among the most important questions you can ask yourself, not only as a social impact communicator but especially as a human being.

In this chapter, I invite you to take a long view. It might seem unpleasant, but it would be even more troubling to avoid thinking about your influence on others. Don't do your life, including the important, purpose-driven work on your plate, on accident.

Some of the most heartbreaking conversations I've had involved friends, team members, and leaders I respect reflecting on things they wish they'd done sooner, or differently, or avoided altogether.

Regret is common to all of us. But in this, our final chapter together, I make the case that you can future-proof your career to mitigate its effects. No matter what happens in the unpredictable future, you can build a life in which you are satisfied with what you have accomplished. Not only that, you can achieve deep contentedness with the person you have become. You can show up for yourself and for those around you.

Legacy seems deeply personal. It is, in a sense. But in other respects, legacy is about the impression you leave on those around you—your family, your friends, and your colleagues at work. The customers and audiences and clients you serve watch you day in and day out. Your legacy imprints on them, for better or for worse.

All of us have rough days, and there are some details of our past we'd just as soon carve out of our legacies. Yet I am convinced that if you approach and design your legacy thoughtfully, the outcome will be a gift to everyone who interacts with you, even on your worst days.

CHAPTER 7 SECRET #7: HIGHLY EFFECTIVE SOCIAL IMPACT COMMUNICATORS ... BUILD PERSONAL AND PROFESSIONAL LEGACIES THAT OUTLIVE THEM AND THEIR CAREERS

Let's learn together how you can create a legacy that outlives you. Leave your sad trombone on the counter because we won't be needing it. This will be fun!

First principles of legacy building for social impact communicators

Before we tackle the how-to of legacy building, let's start by addressing the question: Why would you want to purposely design a legacy as a social impact communicator? I think the reasons might be as different as the sand on the seashore, though the motivation to be intentional with legacy is universal.

Once, a business partner of mine explained the very specific reason he enjoyed the leadership role in his organization. It gave him the confidence to look his children in the eye and tell them honestly that he'd done everything he could to build a better world for them. He spoke in the context of a changing climate and the many environmental challenges our world faces. I suspect his rationale strikes a chord with you, as it did with me.

Whether you have children or not, the idea of leaving things in better shape than we found them is common across families and industries. The farmers with whom I have spent many years working recognize that if their land is managed poorly, the viability of their businesses and their assets becomes deeply uncertain.

That's not a future anyone wants.

This brings us to the first principles of legacy building.

CHAPTER 7   SECRET #7: HIGHLY EFFECTIVE SOCIAL IMPACT COMMUNICATORS ... BUILD PERSONAL AND PROFESSIONAL LEGACIES THAT OUTLIVE THEM AND THEIR CAREERS

Principle No. 1: Legacy is the ripple effect of our actions

You don't have to believe in the butterfly effect to understand that you don't live in a vacuum. What you say, what you do, and how you react to the circumstances you're handed all influence others. You can be a cheery person, or a cranky one, or a seesaw of thoughts and feelings depending on the hour of the day. We all are.

Beyond your own conduct, you have an implicit social contract with others. You agree to advance your employer's mission or, if applicable, to advance the mission of an organization you founded. Consequently, your words and decisions reflect positively, neutrally, or poorly on that organization. You are intractably bound together, even though you remain your own unique person.

Your legacy is especially acute within your family. You are an emissary for the kind of life you've helped build for your spouse or your children, or for yourself alone, or for your dog, Scruffy. The kinds of activities you enjoy, the places you go on vacation, the decisions you make about what you will or won't tolerate. These are pieces of your legacy, and they are bound up in relationship with other people.

In your neighborhood, perhaps you are known as the person who always smiles and waves, or the one who always lends a hand, or the person who covers his head with an umbrella and avoids contact with outsiders. Our actions ripple outwardly and define the nuances of our legacy.

Are your ripples smooth or choppy? If I'm being honest, I probably have some of both emanating from my actions and my character over the years. The more intentional we can get about our legacy, the more we can control the kinds of ripples that wash into people around us.

CHAPTER 7   SECRET #7: HIGHLY EFFECTIVE SOCIAL IMPACT COMMUNICATORS ... BUILD PERSONAL AND PROFESSIONAL LEGACIES THAT OUTLIVE THEM AND THEIR CAREERS

Principle No. 2: Legacy is shiftable, not set in stone

One of the greatest tragedies I can imagine would be to go about my life and career as if I had no choice. You might have experienced great trauma or tragedy in your life. You might have faced unbelievable odds, things I can scarcely imagine. Or you might have lived a plum life.

Whatever highs or lows you face, you have the opportunity now to adapt, adjust, and amend your legacy in the days and months ahead. You can choose to pursue Option A today and then pivot to Option B tomorrow if circumstances change.

If I am unhappy with my attitude in editorial team meetings today, I can try something new tomorrow in an effort to be a better leader and team player. If I stumbled and said something I regret today, I can quickly seek forgiveness and say something encouraging and uplifting tomorrow. I can even pick up the phone or stop by my colleague's desk and make it right immediately.

An unpleasant and flat-out wrong narrative in America today (perhaps in your country's society, too) is that society is divided into two camps: the right-doers and the wrong-doers. The wrong-doers must be kept in line, called to task, and chastised by the right-doers. We all think of ourselves as right-doers, even though our actions often contradict this fanciful belief.

Perhaps this is influenced by politics, a more ancient us-versus-them mindset, or simply by which direction the wind is blowing.

You and I don't have to live this way. Life is too short and too full of promise to let ourselves quickly sort and write off whole segments of humankind. Each of us has permission to design a legacy and to make it more generous and kind and meaningful. It's as true for you as it is for your neighbor.

You can change and grow. So can they. Let's give each other room to do so.

Principle No. 3: Legacy exists beyond our lifetime

Sometimes, it seems like the world is crashing down around your shoulders. Maybe you're on an impossible deadline for a multimillion-dollar project. Perhaps you've just seen a headline that we've yet again notched the hottest month on record as a global community.

In times like these, it's easy to laser focus on the bad news right in front of you. I can't control what happens after I'm gone, you might say to yourself. But I can for sure control what I do this afternoon, this week, or this month to make sure this project gets completed, or this campaign gets launched, or I do my small part to stave off disaster. And well you should.

But it's also important to remember the compounding effect of those actions, on your colleagues and your family, and how they will collectively be remembered and acted upon after you are gone.

None of us knows when our time will come. Death visits all of us no matter how hard we try to duck into an alley to avoid it. So decide the next step to take not merely based on how it helps yourself today, but also on how it helps others tomorrow.

Principle No. 4: Legacy can be a blessing or a byword

I suppose that when you and I are gone, we won't worry anymore about what people thought of us. At that point, the history books have been written. Or, if not a book, at least plenty of loose-leaf paper full of notes about our heritage.

But while you are still living and breathing this beautiful stuff we call oxygen, you have the opportunity to leave a mark that people remember positively. Rather than treating people with haste, as if their problems and needs matter little, you can treat them as if they are the center of your universe. Rather than focusing on what you can get out of a business partnership, or the credit you could get for leading that next campaign, look for opportunities to give credit away.

You can't control what other people think of you or how they interpret your actions, it's true. Yet as much as you can, look for ways to be a gift to those around you. That kind of legacy, and others' desire to mirror that legacy in their own lives, is profound.

Principle No. 5: Legacy persists in the background

Sometimes, when our loved ones pass on and the years progress, we think about those individuals less and less. Other people and events arise to command our attention.

That doesn't mean our loved ones disappear forever. In fact, it doesn't take much to bring their memory and their legacy rushing back. You might peruse a photo album, for example, or see an object they once held dear, or hear a song, or smell something baking and remember how much they loved it.

Our influence lives on, as do our catchphrases, our attitudes, and our ability to make people feel good about themselves. This is true even though the projects we lead at work will transform and evolve long beyond our short careers.

As motivational speaker Myles Munroe once said:

> *Success without a successor is failure. So your legacy should not be in buildings, programs, or projects, your legacy must be in people.*

CHAPTER 7   SECRET #7: HIGHLY EFFECTIVE SOCIAL IMPACT COMMUNICATORS ... BUILD PERSONAL AND PROFESSIONAL LEGACIES THAT OUTLIVE THEM AND THEIR CAREERS

How you can create a legacy that outlives you

Now that you and I are clear on some of the first principles of legacy building for social impact communicators, we can turn to your legacy specifically. When people ask me about the kind of legacy I want to leave, I tend to stumble around and move the toe of my shoe around in the dirt.

For one thing, it can be embarrassing to talk about the kind of stellar person you want to be, or about the accomplishments you desire to achieve, when your dreams and destinations seem so far-fetched. At times, your description of your future self can seem so foreign compared to the person you are today.

My challenge to you, then, is this: dream a little bit. Be proud of the person you are becoming. Imagine what's possible. You only get one chance at this, after all.

I think about my own legacy in several buckets. You might measure your life in similar terms. Feel free to jot down some thoughts on the important components of your life as you scan mine:

- **Spirituality:** My daily faith journey, culminating in a victorious life.

- **Family:** My wife and children and extended family, the people I adore and am pouring into daily.

- **Friends:** People near and far whom I care deeply about—those whose company, wisdom, mentorship, counsel, and encouragement buoy me.

- **Career:** The circles of influence in my technical craft and leadership, including past employers, present clients, and the many other talented people I've been privileged to meet and work with over the years.

- **Communities:** All of the groups of people who share my passion for a particular issue, topic, or hobby.

- **Contributions:** The things I'm leaving behind me like breadcrumbs for future generations to pick up and use. It might be a book, or a sermon, or a meaningful conversation, or a handkerchief. I get to decide!

How do you define the contours of your legacy? This is a deeply personal topic, so take your time considering the question. No one gets to orchestrate the legacy you're leaving behind but you.

Spend time journaling on the topic and pondering what you're leaving behind—not just in your final hour, but during each day as you serve in the capacity of social impact communicator. Remember, your influence as a technically skilled writer, editor, or project manager is important. Yet you are more than that. You are a leader in the purest sense, someone with the capacity to encourage and help people focus and advance important, mission-driven work.

Give yourself the gift of time to reflect on everything you're doing. To encourage you on this journey, I've dedicated the next several pages to sharing with you some of the insights I've gleaned on my own journey as a purpose-driven professional.

These legacy builders, as I call them, can make the process of defining your legacy more satisfying. It can also add breadth and depth to your legacy, turning it into a more accurate reflection of you and your strength of character.

Legacy Builder 1: Give away your grace and mercy liberally

My first observation is the way you show up for those around you matters. This includes your team at work and at home.

CHAPTER 7 SECRET #7: HIGHLY EFFECTIVE SOCIAL IMPACT COMMUNICATORS … BUILD PERSONAL AND PROFESSIONAL LEGACIES THAT OUTLIVE THEM AND THEIR CAREERS

Grace and mercy are increasingly in short supply. We have less patience—and time, it seems—for giving people the benefit of the doubt. In my own country, for example, the gun safety advocacy group Everytown USA reports that road rage shootings are on the rise.[1] We are quick to act in haste, to uncover or even try to correct a multitude of sins, even when the stakes are seemingly much lower—such as at the office.

It's true there are times you must stand up and defend yourself, or push back against sloppy work or decisions that could be costly. Yet you have the choice to do so with grace and mercy.

My guidance is to treat people around you as part of your extended family. When you operate with this framework in mind, you tend to have a much different attitude—about the words you choose to say, about the projects you take on, and about the actions you apply to demonstrate where your heart and values lie.

Grace is the act of extending hope and healing to others. Mercy, meanwhile, is so many things rolled into one, especially forgiveness and compassion.

Be kind to others and to yourself. Recognize the beauty of what you are becoming and of what you and your social impact team are building together.

We get so caught up competing in the track-and-field of daily life that we seldom look up to see where we've been and where we're going.

Be abundantly generous. It's fine if you've built financial wealth, but focus first on wealth of character. Give away as much as you can every single day.

---

[1] "Road Rage Shootings Are Continuing to Surge." March 20, 2023. Burd-Sharps, Sarah, et al. https://everytownresearch.org/reports-of-road-rage-shootings-are-on-the-rise/

CHAPTER 7   SECRET #7: HIGHLY EFFECTIVE SOCIAL IMPACT COMMUNICATORS ... BUILD PERSONAL AND PROFESSIONAL LEGACIES THAT OUTLIVE THEM AND THEIR CAREERS

Legacy Builder 2: Guard your time and share it so it aligns with your values and the mission

Walking through life can feel like trying to dodge a crew of kindergarteners with vacuum cleaners. On every corner, someone is standing at the ready to siphon off chunks of your time, a few minutes here, an hour there. Before you know it, the day is finished, and you're exhausted and keenly away you didn't invest all those available moments exactly as you intended.

It's easy to lose sight of the brevity of everything we see around us. If we don't guard our time and feed it into the people and activities we care most about, we wake up one day to discover it has slipped through our fingers. I don't want that for you, and I certainly don't think *you* want that for you.

How do you right this wrong? First, by guarding your time. Audit your calendar, whether the one on your wall, in a planner, or on an app.

Consider how much autonomy you have. Do you get to control what you do, or does it feel as though your schedule is not your own? There are, of course, trade-offs we make. Your organization and your team need you. That requires a lot of your time as a social impact professional. If you have young children or parents living at home, you're naturally going to spend more time than others on parenting and caretaking activities.

But there might be more freedom and flexibility than you realize. An audit can uncover this. For example, are there things you spend time doing that drive you crazy—that don't serve the legacy you're building? What might you do to reduce or eliminate those activities altogether?

If you have a dream, goal, or project in mind but can never seem to find the time, what would it take to get there? Would you be willing to spend a few early mornings over a brief burst of time to make big progress? What would it mean for your peace of mind and for future generations? What gifts are bottled up inside of you that the rest of us need?

CHAPTER 7   SECRET #7: HIGHLY EFFECTIVE SOCIAL IMPACT COMMUNICATORS ... BUILD PERSONAL AND PROFESSIONAL LEGACIES THAT OUTLIVE THEM AND THEIR CAREERS

As Full Focus founder and chairman Michael Hyatt has written, "Insufficient resources are *never* the main challenge in achieving your dreams."

Think creatively about how to more strategically pursue your priorities. Align your time with your values and your mission.

Then, get after it.

Legacy Builder 3: Be honest with yourself and others about who you really are

Our differences can often be our greatest strengths. This is especially true among social impact teams, as you've seen throughout this book. Diverse teams provide us with renewable energy and give us hope that we're making progress.

Yet you need to show up as your real self, not as the make-believe composite other people might wish you to be. And you have permission to change with time.

I've decided to switch my focus and how I show up throughout my social impact career. At one time, I put a lot of stock in the title I held. To me, earning the position of vice president reflected my experience, my ability to lead, and the blood and sweat I'd put into my work. It was an incredible gift, I was grateful to the mentors who made it possible, and I made every effort to show up as the leader I wanted to be for others.

With time, my focus shifted away from my title and onto my time and the creative ways I wanted to spend it. I discovered that I enjoy entrepreneurship—building businesses, figuring out the keys to success, getting to know new industries and disciplines. I even enjoyed financials, building budgets, and raising money, things that would have made my past self shudder back when I believed math wasn't my strong suit.

You are on your own journey, and you may undergo similar changes in mindset. Those changes can sway how you do your work and spend your time.

CHAPTER 7   SECRET #7: HIGHLY EFFECTIVE SOCIAL IMPACT COMMUNICATORS … BUILD PERSONAL AND PROFESSIONAL LEGACIES THAT OUTLIVE THEM AND THEIR CAREERS

If you decide a leadership role is what you desire—a position that helps you guide the direction and actions of your organization's social impact work—spend time with your leadership team exploring the possibilities. I've been blessed in my career to work under incredible leaders who poured into me their experiences, the nuances of leadership, the difficult decisions that must be made, and the thrill of building something from scratch. Without them, I wouldn't have had the courage to start my own business.

Your adventure might involve a new title, a new job, or simply a change of scenery. Or maybe you want to start something new like I did.

Be who you really are. Living authentically and on purpose is among the greatest gifts you can give to yourself and to those around you who need what only you can give them.

Legacy Builder 4: Focus on actions that hold true 500 years from now

Rarely do we think about how a decision we make today could be interpreted five years in the future, much less 500. Yet if you start filtering your actions through this type of long-term vision, I believe it will serve you, your organization, and your mission well.

You might be thinking, "What a joke! The vast majority of events that happened 500 years ago have been lost to history or shoved onto a bookshelf to collect dust. Why act with a 500-year time horizon in mind?"

The reason is this: the more we consider the downstream impacts of what we do now, the more likely we are to adopt a discipline of thoughtful decision-making.

As communicators, we are frequently up against a tight deadline, so this does not come naturally. I can't count the number of times I've had to quickly whip together a headline and an article, blog post, news release, or event agenda. I bet you can relate. To make matters more complex, you

CHAPTER 7 SECRET #7: HIGHLY EFFECTIVE SOCIAL IMPACT COMMUNICATORS ... BUILD PERSONAL AND PROFESSIONAL LEGACIES THAT OUTLIVE THEM AND THEIR CAREERS

are tired, your supervisor checks in hourly for status updates, and your child has a ball game you can't miss. This is called life, and it happens all the time, even though it can feel like a blur. You just shoulder your way through, clenching your teeth all the while.

But what if you stopped and asked yourself the question: What would happen if I gave these campaign deliverables just one extra hour? What benefits could emerge in the near term and in 500 years? Well, let's consider, using the example of a communications campaign aimed at helping farmers grow their soil health management skills:

- Your emails, white papers, social media posts, or conference materials might be that much more helpful to farmers in your audience.

- More helpful and clear materials are more likely to resonate with farmers.

- Better uptake of those content pieces you've developed increases the odds they will be acted upon. Farmers might decide to make different decisions about the soil in their farm businesses.

- If more farmers are empowered to steward the soil differently, future generations could benefit from greater availability of topsoil—the richest soil that helps crops grow—as well as from higher levels of carbon sequestration, improved wildlife habitat, and so on. Some preliminary research even suggests healthier soil can contribute to higher nutrient density in food. That could contribute to healthier people.

Wow! Can you see the potential of spending an extra hour with your marketing campaign?

CHAPTER 7   SECRET #7: HIGHLY EFFECTIVE SOCIAL IMPACT COMMUNICATORS ... BUILD PERSONAL AND PROFESSIONAL LEGACIES THAT OUTLIVE THEM AND THEIR CAREERS

You won't get the chance to see the ripple effect of your work 500 years hence. But you can do your level best to give your work the effort it deserves. As a professional communicator, you can lead your team and encourage them to be more strategic. More committed to your collaboration with partner organizations. More dedicated to the causes and actions that will help the people you seek to serve.

Focus on making decisions that benefit your great-great-great-great—well, you get the idea.

Legacy Builder 5: Seek forgiveness over apologies

This probably never happens to you, but it occurs in my life with some frequency: I get so caught up in my work, or so focused on balancing a half-dozen projects, that I trip up and make a mistake.

For example, I am a reformed ask-for-feedback-and-act-anyway offender. I used to get so caught up in my work that I'd ask a supervisor or a colleague for input. Then, I'd go ahead and get started on the project anyway. When my supervisor came back and redirected me, I felt shame for having failed to take a breath and regret for having to redo my work because I hadn't done it right the first time.

Mistakes and errors—in our copy, our leadership of a meeting, or our relationship building—leave us feeling like impostors. They make us question whether we should be doing what we're doing. Should we hand over the keys and give up our social impact communication driver's licenses? Is it time for the next generation to take over the ship?

This kind of guilt used to prompt an immediate reaction in me: apologies. I'd go to my supervisor or colleague, explain what I'd done and how I messed up, apologize, and promise to do everything I could so it didn't happen again. I walked away not feeling particularly inspired to take the next step. I lived in fear that at any moment, I could mess up and be back in this predicament.

CHAPTER 7   SECRET #7: HIGHLY EFFECTIVE SOCIAL IMPACT COMMUNICATORS ... BUILD PERSONAL AND PROFESSIONAL LEGACIES THAT OUTLIVE THEM AND THEIR CAREERS

I still have moments of embarrassment, but I've learned over the years to approach mistakes differently. These days, I seek forgiveness rather than offering apologies.

You might find this freeing. Here's why.

First, seeking forgiveness gives you autonomy. It makes you the owner of what happened, even if some or even many aspects of a situation are outside your control. You do not make excuses. You acknowledge what happened and seek to make it right.

Second, seeking forgiveness invites others into your life. It unashamedly spotlights your imperfections and humanity. No one enjoys admitting errors. But the more we do, the more we bond. We are human. We mess up. We need a community that cares enough to listen, acknowledge, embrace us, and move on so that we can get back to contributing to the mission.

Third, forgiveness comes with a call to action. When I ask for forgiveness, I am requesting a response from another person: Will you forgive me? It invites them to give us another chance. Never seek forgiveness out of selfish ambition or the desire to quickly patch over a grievous mistake. Instead, seek it from a place of humility and sincerity, seeking healing and a fresh start.

When you do this, you have a greater appreciation for your progress in the face of adversity. You have greater empathy for everyone around you who, together, makes the extraordinary possible.

Legacy Builder 6: Be slow yet deliberate, not fast and reckless

By now, you are beside yourself. "Slow? Are you kidding? We don't have endless amounts of time to reverse climate change. We've got to get to it!" I agree you should move apace and keep pushing forward, whatever your mission.

CHAPTER 7   SECRET #7: HIGHLY EFFECTIVE SOCIAL IMPACT COMMUNICATORS … BUILD PERSONAL AND PROFESSIONAL LEGACIES THAT OUTLIVE THEM AND THEIR CAREERS

That said, I've seen too many business leaders make the mistake of prioritizing speed over stewardship. They say and do things that are out of character because they are under tremendous pressure to perform. They hyperfocus on important details such as finances or deadlines while losing sight of equally important emotional intelligence priorities such as encouraging colleagues and recognizing good work. This can result in project rework and in interpersonal friction.

The good news is this is largely (admittedly, not entirely) avoidable with a slow yet deliberate mindset. You strive to approach every conversation with colleagues, every decision, and every partnership with calm and thoughtfulness. When the tension and the drama start to ramp up on your team or in your organization, you take a deliberate step back. You consider what makes sense for the mission, the organization, your team, and yourself.

This is especially true when everyone else simply wants you to make a snap decision. Resist. Speed kills, as the saying goes. A slow and deliberate approach buys you valuable time to make a more informed decision. It also earns the respect of others who similarly want to be more strategic and compassionate in their approach to life and relationships.

Legacy Builder 7: Bring trusted partners into your inner circle

On your own, you can't achieve most of the bold and ambitious things staring at you from your to-do list—or your Big Life Goals list.

I know from firsthand experience this isn't an easy lesson to hear. For those of us who are introverts, the idea of battling the world's ills singlehandedly, from the comfort of our favorite room, is appealing. (Bonus points if your room has books, coffee, and a view of rolling hills and farm fields. And a lock!)

This isn't reality, though. You depend on the incredible contributions of your teammates, your leaders, and your partners. Together, you can have an outsized positive impact, whether you work to address climate change, improve racial equity, or build healthier communities. You do so by tapping into collective expertise, passion, joy, and camaraderie.

You do not need to invite everyone into your inner circle. Only welcome the people who build you up, challenge you to be your best, and catch you when you fall. I'm not suggesting that you give everyone else the cold shoulder or that you refuse to work with others. That kind of attitude is unkind, short-sighted, and a fast track to nowhere. Be open to working with, and productively engaging, all kinds of people.

But when it comes to soliciting input about the direction of your life and career—the stuff your legacy is made of—be meticulous. Select high-caliber people who are in your corner advising you and lifting you up. Commit to doing the same for them. Your legacy is built in a community with others. How else will we know the person you are, and the person you are becoming, if you don't hone those superpowers in collaboration with others?

The people you trust most to guide your legacy-building journey can become lifelong friends, business collaborators, mentors, and empathizers.

Leave the comfort of your room. See what you can do together.

Legacy Builder 8: Help others remember the promise of their own multigenerational dream

As you build your own legacy, relishing the idea that what you do today brings value to future generations, help your friends and colleagues remember the importance of their own legacy.

CHAPTER 7   SECRET #7: HIGHLY EFFECTIVE SOCIAL IMPACT COMMUNICATORS ... BUILD PERSONAL AND PROFESSIONAL LEGACIES THAT OUTLIVE THEM AND THEIR CAREERS

Few of us have a dedicated person sitting on our shoulder (hello, Jiminy Cricket!) and reminding us daily of who we are, what we can become, and how we contribute to the greater good. Take it upon yourself to be this kind of figure for people you care about. Social impact work can be challenging and without immediate reward or evidence of progress. Help people around you remember their potential.

Remind your team in meetings and casual conversations that their work in social impact is making the world a better place. It's influencing how we work, play, and live. Pull a colleague aside to thank them for what they're doing. Share how grateful people will be in years to come because of the contributions they made. Because of tough calls they had to act upon.

Few things about your work as a communicator are easy. And there's always more work to do. But it's sufficient to know that you and I make a difference, day after day, month after month.

Let's care enough about one another to keep hope alive.

Ask the experts: How can social impact communicators build personal and professional legacies that outlive them and their careers?

I could have left you here, sitting on the precipice of this vast thing we call social impact communication, pondering your legacy and the meaning of life. But what kind of a friend would that make me? Instead, I've opted to assemble some encouraging words from some peers you've met along the way—leaders like you who are focused on making meaningful change in their lifetimes.

I asked these experts: What can we do, individually and specifically, to build a legacy we're proud to own? Here's what they shared.

CHAPTER 7 SECRET #7: HIGHLY EFFECTIVE SOCIAL IMPACT COMMUNICATORS ... BUILD PERSONAL AND PROFESSIONAL LEGACIES THAT OUTLIVE THEM AND THEIR CAREERS

First, let me just say that I believe very few social impact communicators do their work with their personal legacy in mind. That said, one of the best ways to create a legacy is to build the thing – the strategy, the process, the methodology – that makes it possible for others to follow. It's almost like clearing a jungle – creating a path where there was none, enabling a view that wasn't previously perceptible, defining the most efficient way to get from Point A to Point B. Oftentimes, the things that are the most complex to figure out look like the simplest things in hindsight. Most legacies seem to fall into that category.

—Deron Johnson

Make sure that you mentor someone who can carry the torch for the area of expertise and interest where you have blazed a trail. Choose that person carefully, because their continued work will be the best extension of your legacy.

—Kent Harrison

I was inspired by Blake Mycoskie (founder of TOMS shoes), and I'm sure other social impact entrepreneurs were inspired by someone else. I think that most people want to do good, but most of the time people are busy and focused on their own stuff and problems. Social impact communicators can show the way, can inspire, and can provide a channel not only for people to help, but also to raise awareness and help to improve empathy. By fostering empathy, communicators aim to create a sense of understanding, compassion, and solidarity, which can lead to increased advocacy and positive changes.

—Martín Casanova

By relentlessly walking the talk. This is a tough job, and you need to be equipped for a marathon rather than a sprint.

—Max Gulde

CHAPTER 7   SECRET #7: HIGHLY EFFECTIVE SOCIAL IMPACT COMMUNICATORS ... BUILD PERSONAL AND PROFESSIONAL LEGACIES THAT OUTLIVE THEM AND THEIR CAREERS

There you have it. Be intentional and have integrity in the work you do and in the systems you build to accelerate momentum over the long term. Lift up others and help them build on your insights and triumphs. Remember, we're all figuring this out one day at a time.

Just look at the impact you're having. You should be extremely proud.

Some final thoughts on legacy and the journey before you

What a journey you've taken! At the start of this book, you acknowledged that the very act of explaining social impact communication can be a tall order. And that's before you unpack all the things that effective social impact communicators do to lead and use their technical craft with excellence.

Now, you have a framework you can use to accelerate your effectiveness in doing purpose-driven work and to build a legacy you're proud to own. Not only that but the people who depend on you—your family, your colleagues at work, partners, and audiences outside your organization—stand to benefit greatly, too. When you show up and apply the secrets of highly effective social impact communicators, you reflect your compassion for others. You show your commitment to making this wonderful, messy, ever-changing world a better place for humankind.

Consider how the things you've learned stack together into your legacy.

First, you explored Secret #1 about how, as a highly effective social impact communicator, you care more about the mission than the words. And yet, the words matter a lot. You learned you are a social impact communicator because you use words to open people's hearts. It's that simple.

CHAPTER 7 SECRET #7: HIGHLY EFFECTIVE SOCIAL IMPACT COMMUNICATORS … BUILD PERSONAL AND PROFESSIONAL LEGACIES THAT OUTLIVE THEM AND THEIR CAREERS

Whether you are a journalist, a marketer, or a communications director for a nonprofit, you seek to carry out a mission that results in real change for others. Language is your tool of choice. You bring tremendous technical skill, and you see what exists today and what could exist in the future. That mission is the driving force behind every extraordinary social impact communicator.

Then you learned how to leverage Secret #2: using your gift as a translator inside and outside of your organization. Your role in your organization means you sit at the crossroads of social change, environmental issues, and other important issues. You also can deftly walk between the science of climate change, for example, and the unique roles various teams and partners play in addressing climate change. You can appreciate where people sit, and you can help them have productive conversations. After all: You are a leader, in addition to being a wordsmith. You see the positive potential of people working together to solve problems. You make it so.

Next, you got clear on your personal values with Secret #3. These values give you a sense of true north. Because you are a highly effective social impact communicator, you both live out your own values authentically and seek to understand and appreciate the values of your organization and the people around you.

Rather than losing heart or giving up when you encounter a conflict of values, you get curious. You seek to better understand the things that motivate each of us, as individuals, as companies, as nonprofits, or as government agencies. There is comfort in understanding values. There's also the potential to see ourselves for who we really are. To face big issues together by finding common ground on which to work. Your legacy can model for others how to find unity when division and rivalry seem strongest.

That led you to Secret #4: you have the ability to tap into the renewable energy that comes from teamwork among peers and friends. You have a knack for encouraging others and reminding them why they're doing this

CHAPTER 7 SECRET #7: HIGHLY EFFECTIVE SOCIAL IMPACT COMMUNICATORS … BUILD PERSONAL AND PROFESSIONAL LEGACIES THAT OUTLIVE THEM AND THEIR CAREERS

work. You can choose to lead by example and remain calm under pressure. Things won't always be easy or clear, but they always are worthwhile. Because you are working in the same direction together.

You might find it tempting to stop there, but sometimes, life happens—yes, even at work! So Secret #5 becomes essential: you can cultivate a mindset that reframes setbacks in your social impact work as the crest of a hill. Approach each new challenge with the confidence you can navigate through it, even if you feel as though you can't go on.

Every hill has its peak and then dips lower into a valley of new opportunities. Recognize that the hills you face eventually crest. When you reach the summit, you have greater visibility into the possibilities up ahead of you and your team. Stop, take a drink of water, and plan your next move. This approach separates the highly effective from the downtrodden.

That doesn't mean things won't get messy, a fact you came to terms with by studying Secret #6. You learned some practical ways to navigate the daily grind, the tough and—dare I say it?—not-so-fun parts of what you do. You do meaningful work, though not all parts of it energize you. But you can successfully complete the progress reports and the meetings; you can enjoy the payoff. You can celebrate as the farmers you serve get more value from better soil health. You can sleep better knowing you helped families experience less pollution and better air quality. You can be grateful for the role you played helping people previously excluded from important conversations secure a seat at the table.

To reach those moments of joy, take your daily work step by step. Focus on maintaining momentum. In Walter Isaacson's stunning biography of Leonardo da Vinci, the author describes how some days, da Vinci showed up to observe a mural, apply a brush stroke, and leave for the day.

Your everyday doesn't need to be a spectacular tour de force. It's sufficient to make the brush stroke and step away, knowing you'll be back tomorrow. Keep your eyes on the mission, and paint the vision of where you're going for your team.

CHAPTER 7 SECRET #7: HIGHLY EFFECTIVE SOCIAL IMPACT COMMUNICATORS ... BUILD PERSONAL AND PROFESSIONAL LEGACIES THAT OUTLIVE THEM AND THEIR CAREERS

Which brings us right back here to Secret #7: building a legacy that outlives you.

Social impact communications as a discipline might be new, particularly in the ways we're applying it today. It works in media and in academic circles, in businesses and in nonprofits and in government agencies. Today, you might run a traditional communications campaign using the latest tools and technologies. Tomorrow, you might apply your technical skill set working with entirely new partners, programs, and platforms. You do work others haven't done before, and that's a beautiful thing. It honors and builds upon the legacy of technical skill and human compassion that social impact leaders before you introduced to the world.

Each day, take time to reflect on a meaningful moment in your past that changed the trajectory of your future forever. Consider just how much you've grown and changed—and imagine with excitement what you might get to do in the future.

Legacy is forged over decades. But those special moments? They give you glimpses of what your legacy will be—and remind you why you're still deep into this important work.

Avoid thinking of legacy building as a burden. Instead, treat it like an investment. Aim for more peak moments and valleys of opportunity to strengthen your relationships and your impact. When you do encounter unanticipated detours, resolve to make them more memorable. See the good in the situation and in the people who help you get through it. Be confident in your ability not only to write or edit but especially to encourage and persuade and nurture.

Your legacy can be whatever you want it to be.

And if you've made it to this point, the greatest secret of all is beginning to dawn on you.

You've got what it takes to be a highly effective social impact communicator.

What's more, you *are* one.

CHAPTER 7   SECRET #7: HIGHLY EFFECTIVE SOCIAL IMPACT COMMUNICATORS ... BUILD PERSONAL AND PROFESSIONAL LEGACIES THAT OUTLIVE THEM AND THEIR CAREERS

Key Questions

- What do you want people to remember about you and your work in 500 years?

- What will be the most lasting thing about what you've done in your career and your life?

- What will people say about social impact communicators in the future? Which ones will have made the biggest contributions to improving our world, and why?

- What's one change you could make in the next 90 days to revolutionize your impact?

- What's stopping you from that change, and what's at stake if you don't make it?

CHAPTER 8

Some helpful resources for social impact communicators

When you wake up tomorrow morning, I want you to leap out of bed and scream, "I get to be a social impact communicator!" Please don't hurt yourself. And keep your voice down. It's probably best to avoid waking your spouse, or the neighbors, or the children, too. (Yes, this includes your fur babies!)

Nonetheless, you've earned the right to be excited about, and proud of, your work. Of the ways you and your team make a difference in people's lives.

To assist you on the day-to-day journey, I've put together a handful of resources that can help.

- **Subscribe to my free email newsletter, *Secrets of Social Impact Communicators*:** You'll get weekly insights from me on a range of relevant topics including social impact content strategy and content creation, cultivating the mindset of a highly effective social impact communicator, and much more. I even throw in grant proposal development tips for those of you who might work in the nonprofit space, or at for-profits considering ways to grow your influence. Simply go to www.SilverMapleStrategies.com and sign up using the brief form. Then watch your inbox for a quick email you'll need to confirm your subscription. Remember to click the button!

- **Sign up for my podcast, *Secrets of Social Impact Communicators with Nate Birt*:** I combine stories, insights, strategies, tips, and interviews with world-class social impact communicators from across industries and around the globe. You'll get weekly wisdom and practical steps to grow your career, impact, and effectiveness as a purpose-driven leader. You'll find it on Apple Podcasts, Google Play, and anywhere else fine podcasts are broadcast.

- **Follow me on LinkedIn:** Throughout the week, I share frameworks social impact communicators can use to navigate their biggest challenges (read: opportunities) at work, obtain the peace of mind they deserve, and remember the positive difference they're making. I also post periodic stories of my family's life on our small farm in Missouri. Come for the insights and stay for the baby turkey photos. Find me at www.LinkedIn.com/in/NateBirt.

- **Get my free downloadable guide, 101 Conversation Starters:** Use these prompts to kickstart your most important meetings, internally or with partners, whether your social impact work involves agriculture and the environment, or other social impact priorities in other industries entirely. Simply substitute the

- subject matter for topics your collaborators care about. Use it to build relationships with the people you serve. Apply it to appreciate more deeply the unique strengths and values each of your team members brings to the table. Grab your copy at `www.SilverMapleStrategies.com/ClimateSmart101`.

- **Send me a note or give me a call:** I love hearing from you, and I'm here to help you continue your journey as a highly effective social impact communicator. Reach out anytime at nate@silvermaplestrategies.com or via my cellphone at 573-591-1990 if you have an observation, a question, or a problem you're trying to solve. I'm happy to help.

Recommended Reading

If you're looking to level up your learning and capacity for change, there is a wealth of great insight available online and in print. Here are some resources I recommend:

- **B The Change:** This regularly updated resource highlights stories and strategies from B Corporations and other leaders making a difference in the world in a variety of areas including racial equity and climate action. Sign up at `http://bthechange.com` or look for their content on Medium.

- **Center for Social Impact Communication:** Georgetown University offers a wealth of research reports, events, and even a certification for social impact communicators of all backgrounds. To learn more, visit `http://csic.georgetown.edu`.

CHAPTER 8 SOME HELPFUL RESOURCES FOR SOCIAL IMPACT COMMUNICATORS

- **Edward R. Murrow Center for Media & Health Promotion Research:** Washington State University researchers are studying new ways to engage the human brain with media for positive outcomes in a range of areas including civic engagement, the environment, and human health. To learn more, visit http://murrow.wsu.edu.

- *The Aspirational Business:* In this information-packed book, GivingSpring founder and president Dora Lutz, an ESG expert and strategist, walks you and your organization through the process of strategically evaluating the change you seek—and then creating an action plan to integrate that strategy across your organization. As Lutz writes, "Often we know that we can take action, we don't always have the knowledge we need to bring it to life." This book provides the knowledge you need to get to work, quickly and effectively.

- Last but not least, I encourage you to use your search engine of choice to scan for new articles, books, and resources for leaders who do the kind of social impact communication you do every day. Try phrases such as "CSR communication," "ESG communication," and "social impact communication." You can also try prompting the generative AI tool of your choice for a list of relevant social impact communication resources specific to your industry, interest area, or organization.

Index

A

Accountability, 16, 94
Adaptability, 161
Anxiety, 51, 102, 154, 155
Attention
    capturing, 152, 153
    framework, 153, 154
    language, 154
    messy situation, 153
    projects, 153
    significance, 152
    worship service, 152

B

Business partner, 159, 165, 169

C

Clients, 10, 15, 16, 41, 47, 53, 141
Climate change, 22, 29, 37, 39, 58, 65, 86, 111, 140
Climate-change communication, 29
Climate-change program, 140, 159
Communication professionals, 6
Compassion, 21, 52, 58, 60, 64, 67, 92, 93, 99, 108
Confidence, 4, 7–9, 52, 55, 100, 118, 133
Consumer audience, 8
Conversationalist, 11
Conviction, 58
Corporate communications team, 26
Crest of a hill, 109–111
    crest-climbing insights, 116–123
    effective social impact communicators, 122, 123
    act with integrity, 124
    lead with humility, 125
    openness and transparency, 127, 128
    scientific approach, 125, 126
    stay skeptical, 127, 128
    navigated challenges, 129–132
    "S" curve, 113
    watchout and opportunity, 133, 134
Curiosity
    courage/creative, 14
    joy, 13
    lower stress, 12
    questions, 12

INDEX

D
Darker values, 58
Diverse teams, 174

E
Empowering, 62, 64, 66, 110
Entrepreneurship, 136, 174
External communications, 29, 67

F
Facilitating, 65
Faithful, 53
Farmers, 165
Fear, 59
Fear into compassion, 60
Frustration, 12

G
Gratitude, 101, 102
Guilt, 12, 144, 177

H
Hesitation, 59, 60
Higher Calling, 58, 60, 64, 66
Honor, 39, 53, 56, 60, 143, 157
Humor, 53

I
Information paralysis, 155
Innovate-as-we-go approach, 96
Innovation, 53
Integrity, 53, 70, 123, 124, 183

J
Journalism, 141

K
Kindness, 53, 65, 74, 103, 124

L
Leadership, 54, 92, 107
Legacy, 164
    contours, 171
    experts, 181, 183
    framework, 183
    issues, 184
    journalist, 184
    life's components, 170, 171
    mindset, 185
    moments of joy, 185
    opportunities, 185
    personal values, 184
    renewable energy, 184
    social impact communications, 186
    social impact communicator, 171
    stellar person, 170
    translator, 184
Legacy builders
    actions, 175–177
    forgiveness/apologies, 177, 178

grace and mercy, 172
help, friends and colleagues, 180
honesty, 174, 175
slow/deliberate mindset, 179
time, 173, 174
trusted partners, 179, 180
Legacy building principles
existence, lifetime, 168
history books, 168
memory/legacy, 169
opportunity, 167
people's thought, 168, 169
ripple effect, actions, 166
tragedies, 167
Less-than-optimal values, 54
Live events, 142

M

Meetings/email conversations, 140
Messy
circumstances, 140
definition, 137
progress reports, 137–139
Mission
anchor, 6
defining process, 4
framing, 5
social impact, 6

N

Non-social impact, 139
Nurture, 53, 58, 64, 66, 67, 94, 186

O

Organization holds values, 55
Organization's values, 52, 73

P, Q

Panic into peaceful action, 154, 156
Personal values, 71, 75
Physical education, 14
Planning fallacy, 85
Predictability, 158, 161
Procrastination methods, 143

R

Regular conversations, 159, 160
Relatability, 92
Revolutionary War period, 2

S

Satisfied persistence
around in circles, 144
authority mismatch, 146
bandwidth mismatch, 144
capability mismatch, 148
circular motion, 149
definition, 141
live events, 142
matrix mismatch, 145
messy, 144
scheduling mismatch, 147
sideways motion, 144
social impact efforts, 142

INDEX

Satisfied persistence (*cont.*)
   social impact successes, 142
   social impact valuation mismatch, 148, 149
   tie up, loose ends, 143
   track metrics, 144
   urgency mismatch, 145
Scientific approach, 125
"S" curve, 113
Self-aware, 15
Self-doubt, 112
Self-preservation, 59
Self-Preservation to nurture, 60
Silent moments, 156–158
Skepticism, 127
Social impact, 139
Social impact assignment
   alternative approaches, 11, 12
   ask experts, 11
   commit emotions to memory, 10
   humanity, 13
   issue, 11
Social impact communications, 7, 23, 112, 139, 141, 155, 186
   burnout, 81–83
   complex issue, 36, 37
   government agencies, 32
   industries, 45
   issue, 34, 35
   multistakeholder, 31
   nonprofits, 32
   partnership, 40, 41
   peer groups, 46
   personal views, 38, 39
   private-sector, 31
   skilled translators, 47, 48
   stakeholder types, 33
   stay focused, 41, 42
   teamwork, 43, 44
Social impact communicator, 4, 8, 15, 114
   building, 63
   capacity, 171
   choices, 69
   collaboration, 70
   compromise values, 68
   definition, 136
   editing, 61
   empowering, 62
   facilitating, 62
   intentions/goals, 73, 74
   key values, 64
   leading, 62
   personal values, 75
   procrastination methods, 143
   resources, 189
      The Aspirational Business, 192
      B Corporations, 191
      email newsletter, 189
      Georgetown University, 191
      guide, 190
      LinkedIn, 190
      podcost, 190
      Washington State University, 192
   scenarios, 71
   sets goals, 69
   values conflict, 72

workshop, 68
writing, 61
Social impact community, 8, 9
Social impact entrepreneur, 19, 182
Social impact journey,
    47, 70, 74, 139
Social impact mission, 83, 136, 149
    children/professionals, 21
    climate change, 22
    leadership team, 20, 21
    opportunities, 18, 19
    recognize, 17
    risks, 17
Social impact professionals, 142
Social impact programs, 78
Social impact projects
    amount of dust, 151
    Dust Bowl pictures, 149
    dust storms, 150
    dustups, 150
    experts, 150, 151
    issues, 150
Social impact team
    micro habits, 94–106
    PURSUE framework
        enthusiastic, 91–93
        positive attitude, 89
        relatable, 90
        stalwart, 90
        understandable, 89
        useful, 91
    strategies for strengthening
        celebrate statistics, 87, 88
        conduct meetings, 84

"go big or go home"
    philosophy, 86, 87
    hopes and dreams, 85
    set deadlines, 85, 86
Social impact teams, 174
Social impact work, 111, 115, 117,
    122, 125, 129, 133, 140, 181
    watchout and opportunity,
        133, 134
Social media, 91, 95, 99
Sorrow to higher calling, 60
Stewardship, 58
Stress, 154
Subsistence into stewardship, 60

T, U

Teamwork, 107, 108
Technical skills, 7
Traditional communications, 111
Translational communication
    skills, 37
Translational communicator,
    27, 29, 30
Transparency, 123, 128

V

Values, 52
Vision, 54, 140

W, X, Y, Z

Weeklong project, 164
Work ethic, 53

GPSR Compliance

The European Union's (EU) General Product Safety Regulation (GPSR) is a set of rules that requires consumer products to be safe and our obligations to ensure this.

If you have any concerns about our products, you can contact us on

ProductSafety@springernature.com

In case Publisher is established outside the EU, the EU authorized representative is:

Springer Nature Customer Service Center GmbH
Europaplatz 3
69115 Heidelberg, Germany

www.ingramcontent.com/pod-product-compliance
Lightning Source LLC
LaVergne TN
LVHW010340260326
834688LV00036B/801